Alchemy

Alchemy
The Material World of David Adjaye

Spencer Bailey

Foreword
Teresita Fernández

As a conceptual artist who makes work about place, landscape, and wayfinding, I have always thought of material as a touchstone that connects our earthly presence to both the subterranean and the cosmos. The raw materials that we take out of the ground are critical to our built environments, but are also profoundly connected to our collective mythologizing, dreaming, and imagining. I relish the idea of the elemental as plant, animal, or mineral, and the implied role of the artist as someone designated to invoke images out of the very essence of the world. Gold, wood, malachite, onyx, lapis lazuli, marble, and iron ore—these materials are, literally, pieces of places. Everything we know about our physical location is just matter, transferable and mutable.

It is no coincidence that the word *material* shares the same etymological root with the words *matter*, *maternal*, and *matrix*. Its connection to the generative life force is inseparable. The word *matrix* means "womb," and is also the geological term used to describe the fine-grained background material in which a gem, a fossil, or a metal is lodged or hidden. It is derived from the word *mā* in Sanskrit, meaning both "mother" and "measure." In this way, we measure the physical world through the very substance that both gives birth to it and generates it until it de-materializes back into itself—a perpetual process of being born, maturing, and being absorbed back into the very stuff of the universe, all while simultaneously bearing witness to this act of creation within our own bodies. The deep red oxidized color and metallic taste of our blood is the result of iron created billions of light years away the moment a distant star died. As human beings, we have always searched to understand where and how we belong in the universe; perhaps this is the reason we've never stopped looking up at the night sky for orientation.

Materials carry an embodied intelligence that is scaleless and timeless, immense and vast, but also intimate, cellular, and crystalline. In our human-centric view of existence, we often lose sight of the fact that we *are* the universe—that it isn't just that we utilize and transform materials as something utilitarian outside of ourselves, but that we are in fact made up of those very materials. In this living alchemy of becoming and unraveling, constructing and dissolving back into ourselves, we participate in the graceful churning of ageless transmutations, forever contracting and expanding as elastic loci of cosmic magic. It is emotional and humbling to recognize our participation in this ancient pattern of recycling.

I've had many conversations with David about the sacred nature of shadows in Japan, the palpable spirit of rocks and ancestral trees, the connection between copper and the planet we call Venus, and our genetic lineage from the stars. As thinkers engaged in the poetics of making, we often speak the same language of the ephemeral and hold mute reverence and awe for the unnamed mysteries that both materials and meaningful emptiness can carry. Perhaps more than that of any other architect of our time, David's unconventional practice generously invites us to learn from the inherent dignity that materials possess. His unique approach to material invention and his eloquently built spaces of self-reflection reminds us that our human consciousness is carefully woven into endless buildings, landscapes, and galaxies within this magnificent matrix. It is in this radical act of alchemy that we become very much like materials; we remember that we are capable of making the earth a more just, balanced, and dignified place of reciprocity when we seek to make constellations of ourselves—luminous and transfigured.

Preface
Sir David Adjaye OM OBE

My entire practice is about the negotiation of meanings and re-meanings of material. When I was studying in Japan in the early 1990s, I saw a profound re-meaning of material within culture: what was considered to be "primitivism" in the West was there transformed into the most significant and sophisticated materials of the world. Earth, mud, sticks, thatch, and a few rocks amalgamated into an architecture that connected to the cosmos and revealed unseen interconnectivity between people and place.

After this experience, I found myself returning to my own roots in Africa. I realized how lucky I was to have been born there. A 360-degree effect occurred: with a turn in the way that I viewed life and materials, my return home meant that I had to re-encounter a past that I was a part of through that lens. I immersed myself in the continent's rich history and inventive power—its magnificent landscapes, geographies, and kingdoms. I discovered that ancient African peoples were masters of what it means to build and commune.

I studied Kemet, the African-centered framing of ancient Egypt, which literally means "black lands"—a reference to the fertile black soils of the Nile, as well as to the Black civilization built alongside it. Through this, I learned the elements of city-making in a different way. In Kemet, city-making wasn't just about infrastructure—that was almost secondary. It was about the earth, spiritual and spatial ritual, reverence, community, and mythos. The city existed and depended entirely upon its relationship to the Nile.

The people of Kemet observed that the Nile would flood for eighty days at a time, which coincided with the heliacal rising of the star Sirius—a key event that led to the creation of their calendar. They didn't try to control or remedy this flooding, but rather to *understand* it. Based on the flooding, the year was divided into three seasons of four months each: *akhet*, or "inundation," which covered the flood period; *peret*, or "emergence," which was a time of planting seeds; and *shemu*, or "low water," which was a time of harvest. The majority of crops were stored in granaries, and the mastering of agriculture led to the beginning of an economic system. In return, they regarded the Nile as a sacred being, often represented as the god Hapi. Offerings would be made along the river. Irrigation and agriculture techniques and tools evolved from this tradition. Through the transportation of water and the use of the earth in building, the city expanded.

Not only did I become fascinated by this history, I discovered that the seven regions of Africa held a blueprint for civilization and how it was sustained. There was a circularity in the way the stories of Africa perpetuated movements. Materials that came from the earth always returned there.

Throughout the 2000s, I undertook a decade-long study of Africa, traveling to all fifty-four capital cities and looking closely at the fundamentals of each, beyond simply historical and architectural traditions. Through that exploration, I gained a greater understanding of the importance of geography and climate in shaping these modern metropolises. Living in Africa now—I moved to Ghana with my family in the fall of 2019—I've been researching it more and more as I immerse myself in it. In particular, I've been looking at the architecture of some of the oldest cultures on earth, such as the San people, a hunter-gatherer tribe in southern Africa, who built domed structures out of sticks and grass in Botswana's Kalahari Desert; the Samburu people, of Nilotic origin, in north-central Kenya, who built huts of mud, hide, and grass strung over poles; and the Musgum, of northern Cameroon, who created conical dwellings from compressed, sun-dried mud. I've also been looking at various ancient structures, including the Ksar Draa, a double-walled building made of clay-bonded stones and located in the Sahara Desert in Algeria; a beehive-like "roundhouse" in Rwanda, constructed of cypress, bamboo, grass, and vegetable fibers; and the Kasubi Tombs in Kampala, Uganda, made of a thick thatched roof that extends down to the ground, supported by wood poles wrapped in bark cloth.

I've become particularly obsessed with the idea of absence, but not in a void-like way. I'm more fascinated with this ancient idea of building *from* the earth, and letting a structure return back to the earth—of using mud, rammed earth, and other materials that can decompose. Things that make a return, full circle, into the earth, back where they came from. We need to move away from what I call a "prejudice of materials"—the hierarchy of materials, or the extraction of materials that are really examples of limitations. When you understand the earth as a continuity, you can see materials as abundant, and not finite, because in that context they exist as a part of a cycle. This cycle may not occur on a human timescale, though. To impose the human timescale would be the Anthropocentric approach to the material.

I believe a negotiation needs to occur. Can we ask ourselves: Okay, we no longer have enough timber in this region at this particular season, so can I build with mud instead? Is there enough earth within my locality to build this? Can I use mud to make a high-rise? From these questions come the ideas, which grow into form, which can then create the habitation. A series of relationships—an *ecology*—comes into play. This is the most pressing thing: how to make an architecture that can simply go back to itself. How to make an architecture that itself can make a return.

In my early work, I was very interested in the novelty of new materials and their performance. I thought lightness was what it was all about—that reuse was a much better way of working. But, over time, I learned that even this was an artifice against nature. Reuse is still a defiance against the cycle of return, because it creates a type of mimicry. It wasn't about switching one material with certain properties for the other. The artifice, or the mimicking of the materiality, is the forced performance of it.

I'm also interested in the creation of a space in which a material can be—from birth to death—a type of sustenance. For me, this is the most radical sustainability. In my early projects, sustainability was about lightness, energy, and luminosity. Beginning with Elektra House (1999), every single one of my projects was concerned with lightness and energy. I always thought that that sort of stewardship and engagement was critical. But it becomes even more radicalized with this idea of a return to earth, of creating an architectural cycle in which the structure itself can be reduced back.

This might very well mean that we have to reckon with and counter the notion of the Anthropocene, which not only presents the human as the dominant way of seeing, but supposes a specific system of the human, which needs things done on a particular timescale. Slow architecture may be what makes sense now. I mean "slow" in the sense of a negotiation. It's about negotiating new elements within the cycle of life, on multiple timescales.

The two fundamental materials used on the continent of Africa are wood and mud. In thinking about that, I'm very interested in how we can make these two foundational materials of habitation relevant in the twenty-first century: how do they relate to the typologies of the contemporary world? Can we develop new technologies of earth or timber architecture toward a more radical sustainable future? The tools I've collected and the lessons I've learned from all the previous kingdoms on the African continent show that the radical sustainable future we desire is possible. At this point of my career, and in this urgent stage of the climate crisis, I'm interested in the dialogue of scarcity that surrounds us, and the areas in which we can find reproduction through scarcity. How we can find new construction from the rubble and work with the cycle of the earth.

I don't agree with all of Buckminster Fuller's ideas, but I've always loved his "Spaceship Earth" concept. The problem was that he was too busy trying to shield humans from the cosmic world, thinking that it was just so bad that we needed to be in a bubble. We don't need to be in a bubble. I'd rather take a toxic world than a bubble. We need to be *in* the earth. To experience it. To be *with* it. We must start from the premise that we're going to work with the earth, research it, investigate it, understand our relationships with and within it, and form a real thesis of engagement from it.

Architecture should now begin with the humility of saying, "All we have is this earth."

Introduction
Spencer Bailey

Perhaps no word better captures the magic of David Adjaye's architecture than *alchemy*. For the architect, alchemy is a material manifesto—a transformative connection point; a portal; a meditative meeting place of space, time, and memory; a merging of architecture, nature, and the cosmos; a celebration of interconnectedness. It is the combination of physical materials with other sensory elements, such as light, sound, air, and smell. It is haptic. It is the humble understanding that, one day, the materials he uses will return to the earth and, by reason of that, must be revered and respected. It is the elevation of both people and the planet through built form. It is an environment's "full and integrated material, embodied, and spiritual essence," as the Finnish architect Juhani Pallasmaa effectively defines it.[1]

Through his adept understanding of materiality, tactility, light and shadow, climate, geography, and atmosphere, Adjaye creates architecture with a conscience. With a knack for crafting profound material/immaterial presence, he has the rare ability to design evocative environments—living, breathing buildings and structures that are full of meaning, sensitivity, and emotional impact. Adjaye achieves this in large part by selecting and, in certain cases, developing and fabricating materials that, when combined and thoughtfully integrated, transform the ordinary into the extraordinary. Adjaye's projects invite introspection and encourage deeper engagement. Those who interact with his buildings are, at one point or another, likely to experience a heightened intensity of feeling, sensorial delight, or even skin sensations—body and mind phenomena the poet and naturalist Diane Ackerman has termed "synaptic junctions."[2]

Through his material intelligence, Adjaye makes meaningful connections and brings new life to neighborhoods, streetscapes, and landscapes. From some of his earliest commissions in London, such as Elektra House (1999) and Dirty House (2002; pages 34–37), to more recent projects such as the McCarter Switching Station (2018; pages 56–63) in Newark, New Jersey, this has always been the case. As is embodied in the ethereal central atrium at the Smithsonian National Museum of African American History and Culture, or NMAAHC (2016; pages 142–52), on the National Mall in Washington, DC, Adjaye turns spaces into warm, contemplative environments that invite a sense of calm, focus, and reflection—and that often relate, in subtle and surprising ways, to their surroundings. With his understanding of how materials may react and respond to light, sound, moisture, and touch, he forms intricate, multilayered architectural experiences. Viewing his buildings in both social and emotional terms, he reshapes perspectives and ways of seeing, but also, even more importantly, ways of *being* and *feeling*.

Underlying all of Adjaye's projects—the central tenet—is luminosity. As a whole, his work could be looked at as an ongoing study into the ways in which light affects form. For Adjaye, light functions as a transformer and a revealer. In many respects, it can be considered a sort of alchemical clock: stand at the right place, at the right time of day, during a particular moment of the year, when the sun hits a certain angle in a certain way, and your perception or consciousness might shift. One material could reveal itself

Elektra House (1999) in London.

to be entirely different than you initially thought, allowing for a new frame of mind, an opening up of alternative perspectives, another way of looking at a space and a place and, perhaps, in turn, the world—without prejudice.

For Adjaye, choosing and using materials is, above all, about understanding and redefining the value system placed on a particular material in the world at large. He views material selection as an exercise—or "design trope"[3]—in understanding the potential of, say, cheap plywood to become something special through refinement and specific alignment. Materials, Adjaye believes, depend as much on the context in which they're installed as they do on their use.[4] Questioning the various codes and meanings that locales, cultures, and societies place upon certain materials, Adjaye forms resonant spaces that elevate and empower, creating, as he describes, "a justice of space."[5]

Through a process of reframing and reshaping, Adjaye turns preconceived understandings of materials and their so-called "values" on their heads. This is perhaps best exemplified by the contrast between his Sugar Hill mixed-use development (2015; pages 46–55) in Harlem, New York, and his first high-rise tower, 130 William (2021; pages 94–101) in Lower Manhattan, both of which are meditations on black-pigmented concrete—one built to be affordable housing; the other, high-end living. With great subtlety, these two buildings elevate the mundane and the everyday through particular respect for the materials at hand. In doing so, they provide deeply rooted, across-time-and-space associations via a heightened sense of materiality. By approaching materials themselves with care, Adjaye in turn brings similar dignity to buildings and their occupants, neighborhoods and their neighbors, and cities and their citizens, no matter the context.

Adjaye's architecture stands out especially for its unexpected material combinations. In his book *Materials and Meaning in Architecture*, the historian and theorist Nathaniel Coleman writes that "joining seemingly irreconcilable materials—perishable wood and durable metal, for example—heightens senses of things by displacing them. Estrangement disrupts expected perception."[6] Adjaye is a shrewd practitioner of such thinking, intermingling materials that on the surface would appear to be opposites or to clash but that, in his hands, when brought together, create profound connections and juxtapositions—at once refreshingly familiar and delightfully otherworldly.

At the entryway of Adjaye's studio at Edison House in London, a beautiful mess of materials is splayed on a shelf, in contrast with a wavy green curtain. While many architecture studios keep material samples like this, typically they're tucked away, or serve as literal palette cleansers, laid out cleanly in rows or tidily pinned up. But this unexpected selection, in its glorious disarray, is nothing like that. There's incredible order within the disorder—a special eye, a specific taste, a particular vision, an artful touch. Even the haphazard way the materials are stacked up on top of or leaning against each other feels just right. The pile itself is, in essence, alchemy.

Simple as it may initially seem conceptually, there is incredible complexity underlying Adjaye's material approach,

A stack of material samples in the Adjaye Associates Edison House studio in London, as seen in 2017.

making it decidedly tricky to pin down. But at its heart is an appreciation of both the tactile and immaterial qualities inherent in a material, as well as their performance aspects, their psychological or "neuroaesthetic" qualities, and their profound mythical, social, and cultural meanings. Also of utmost importance to Adjaye are the ways in which materials connect to geography and origin, as is understanding the life cycle of a material. Bringing a whole-earth mindset to materiality, Adjaye intimately understands the full breadth involved in shaping resonant physical spaces. Alchemy could be considered a crescendo of this thinking.

The notion of alchemy has long been on Adjaye's mind. In a conversation published in 2012, about a Princeton University art and architecture studio he and the Cuban-American artist Teresita Fernández (the author of this book's Foreword) taught together in the late 2000s, the two discussed the subject. Fernández, whose work similarly explores taking ordinary materials and transforming them, told Adjaye that alchemy is "really never about the material," but rather "about the thing that you project on the material," to which Adjaye replied that it isn't so much about changing a material as it is *reframing* it. What Fernández told Adjaye next gets to the heart of Adjaye's work and this book: "[Alchemy is] about layering other things onto it. There's actually no matter to it at all. It's about what's projected onto it, and that is intellectually mental. But it's also emotional, which is an aspect that no one ever wants to talk about, because it's the most difficult thing to talk about, but it is precisely those articulated things that change the matter."[7]

To completely comprehend the material makeup—that is to say, the emotional underpinnings—of Adjaye's buildings and structures requires understanding the Ghanaian British architect himself, and how his peripatetic past led him toward the particular path he's on today. Born in Dar es Salaam, Tanzania, in 1966, to Ghanaian parents, he spent his early life in Africa and the Middle East. Because of his father's work as a diplomat, the family moved around frequently when he was child, from Ghana to Egypt, to Lebanon, and then to Saudi Arabia—all by the time he was 12—before arriving in the United Kingdom in 1979.

For the young Adjaye, this roving period proved incredibly life-giving. One of the earliest memories he recalls is seeing the Egyptian pyramids for the first time, a magical, awe-inspiring experience of material wonder that transfixed his mind around the power of built form. Another memory from these years was of a visit to the historic city of Jeddah, Saudi Arabia. In particular, he remembers Jeddah's traditional compound mud houses, "with walls that were so high that you couldn't see your neighbors; you just saw the sky and whatever was in your nature." The effect those houses had on him was transformative.

Adjaye's nomadic upbringing was also traumatic, often unstable, and compounded by cultural and religious friction. One moment he'll never forget was when he was a young boy, in Beirut, playing on his family's balcony as the Syrian tanks arrived.[8] Adjaye also experienced a harrowing family crisis during these early years: when his father was posted in Ghana, Adjaye's brother Emmanuel, then age 1, fell into a coma after getting a fever and became paralyzed on one side of his body.[9]

Later, while an architecture student at London South Bank University, Adjaye grew frustrated by the lack of dignity and care he witnessed at Emmanuel's school—including the building facilities. This led him to thinking about designing a socially and environmentally conscious structure purpose-built for those with disabilities. In the following years, this concept evolved into his 1993 Royal College of Art (RCA) master's project, a timber-clad carbon-neutral center for disabled people. A revelatory design, the project was also rooted in Adjaye's yearlong experience, in the early 1990s, studying in Japan. There he learned about mass-timber architecture and formed a deep connection to, and understanding of, geography and climate, as well as the sensorial effects of tactility and atmosphere. Spending three seasons in Kyoto, he closely analyzed the angles of the sun and studied its gardens and temples, including the seventeenth-century Katsura Imperial Villa (Japanese architect Arata Isosaki, practically defining alchemy, has called Katsura "a text rich with ambiguity where architectural languages of spatially and temporally different sources are juxtaposed").[10] Adjaye describes his time in Japan as "a profound awakening of material presence"—one that led to his "first awareness that human beings made civilizations that were actually aligned with the seasonality and the cosmology of the world."

David Adjaye
RCA 1993

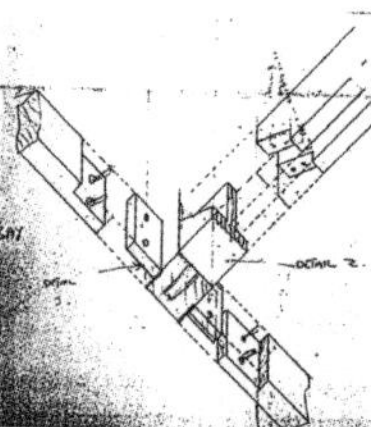

Images of Adjaye's 1993 Royal College of Art master's project, a concept for a timber-clad center for people with disabilities.

A sketch by Adjaye for a design that received the 1993 Royal Institute of British Architects Bronze Medal.

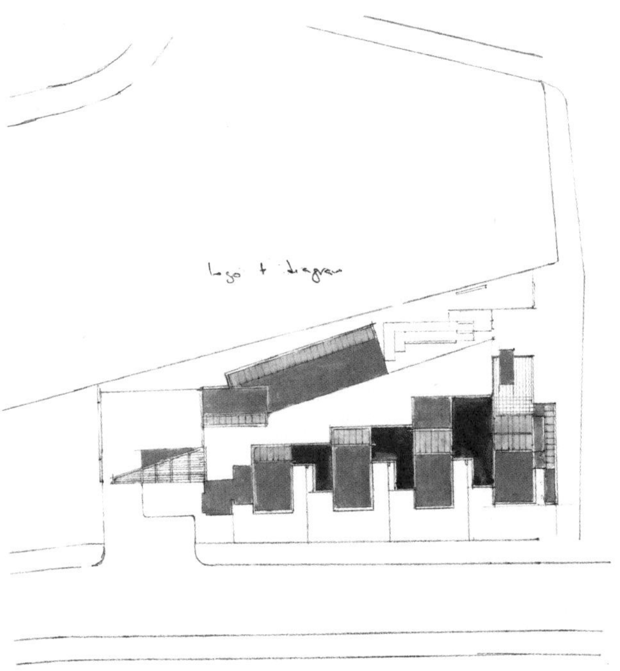

Beyond his stay in Japan, during his years at the RCA, Adjaye frequently traveled around Europe and the Middle East, soaking up both ancient architecture—the Parthenon in Athens, the Pantheon in Rome—and modernist masterworks, such as Le Corbusier's Villa Savoye in Poissy, France. Other early formative experiences included the months he spent working in the offices of David Chipperfield, in London, and Eduardo Souto de Moura, in Portugal. Especially affecting was his time with Souto de Moura, known for his out-of-the-box approaches to architectural methods and materials, and a man who is, as Adjaye puts it, "working on the idiosyncrasies of his mind, working with poetry, working with his own language, working with humor." It was there that Adjaye learned that, within the material and form of a structure, there could be an architectural "joke"—not a punchline, exactly, but rather a wry element that requires you to look closely at a building to truly understand it. A nod. *A wink.* Working for Souto de Moura helped show Adjaye that architecture can have an array of subtle layers embedded within it.

Yet another fortuitous factor of Adjaye's education at the RCA was the opportunity to study under the architects Alison and Peter Smithson. The couple's postwar work, which largely focused on integrating the social, cultural, and environmental fabrics of dense urban cities, explored ideas such as "climate moderation" and the "charged void"—concepts central to Adjaye's practice today. The Aïshti Foundation (2015; pages 134–41) in Beirut, which boldly marks its place along the Mediterranean Sea with a zigzag-patterned red metal facade, is a shrewd model of this. As are earlier projects, such as the glass-walled Idea Store community centers on Chrisp Street and Whitechapel Road (2004 and 2005, respectively; pages 208–13) in the London borough of Tower Hamlets, both the result of Adjaye's first-ever competition win.

The architect and sculptor Theo Crosby, who was a vocal critic of Modernism, was the head of the RCA when Adjaye was a student. He, too, had an effect on Adjaye's thinking. Adjaye fondly remembers a class Crosby taught on the craft of stonecutting:

> Theo hands me a chisel and a hammer and puts a block of limestone in front of me and says, 'Carve a Roman letter.' We [the students] thought it was a joke, so none of us were taking it seriously, but then we tried to do it.... It was completely amazing to have this piece of limestone and to try to just chisel a letter. It numbed us all. Some of us were laughing about it, but I remember thinking, God, that was much deeper than I thought. I thought this was a little bit too juvenile, but actually there was something just a bit—you know, the vibration in your hands, the whole thing. He was trying to *physicalize* architecture for us.

LN House (2008) in Denver, Colorado.

The material heft and weight embodied in so many of Adjaye's buildings—whether LN House (2008) in Denver, Nanjing House (2012; pages 38–45) in China, or the Ruby City art center (2019; pages 64–73) in San Antonio, Texas—is no doubt an outgrowth of this perspective. Architectural em dashes, Adjaye's projects put an emphasis on the physicalization of architecture. They stand strong and proud in their reason for existing.

Though Adjaye was studying architecture, he found himself most drawn to spending time with the art students, and artists would indeed, not so coincidentally, become many of his earliest clients. At the RCA, he interacted with artists and makers who "were asking more fundamental questions [than architects were]—questions addressing morality and social context, and how the maker can and should respond to these questions."[11] Today, Adjaye's architecture reflects this juncture clearly. And were it not for these particular years in London, he says, he would likely never have come to the idea of starting an architectural practice in the first place. His experiences in the UK in the 1980s and early 1990s led him to explore the expansive ways in which the built environment could address issues of social justice through construction and community accessibility. Because of this, his architecture, whether public or private, doesn't impose; it intentionally invites and encourages. It is literally sensitive to its surroundings.

In 1994, Adjaye set up a small office in the East End of London and took on whatever compelling work he could find within the various creative circles he was running in. These jobs included a set for a Pretenders music video, a wine cellar for Pink Floyd guitarist David Gilmour, and a house (never built) for the fashion designer Alexander McQueen. A Noho noodle bar, constructed with polycarbonate, corrugated resin, and steel, received particular public attention and praise. During this time, Adjaye also designed a home and studio for the artist Chris Ofili, who went on to become a close friend and collaborator. Later, Adjaye worked with Ofili on *The Upper Room* (2002), an evocatively lit installation consisting of thirteen of the artist's paintings (now in the permanent collection of the Tate); a 2003 Venice Biennale presentation (pages 201–7); the Stephen Lawrence Center (2007; pages 214–19) in London, technically Adjaye's first memorial; and houses and studios for Ofili in Trinidad and Tobago. Reflecting on this early work, Adjaye has taken note of its "atmospheric quality"[12]—a quality that has remained present ever since.

Adjaye's most notable project from this period was Elektra House, for the artists Giorgio Sadotti and Elizabeth Wright. A windowless lightbox of a structure in London's Whitechapel neighborhood, built with dark phenolic resin-faced timber, it creates a mysterious, satiny sheen across its facade. Unconventional in its material execution, the building adds a tactile edge to the fabric of the street-scape while still embedding itself respectfully within the two- and three-story brick structures surrounding it.

Upon setting up Adjaye Associates in 2000, the architect won the Idea Store commissions. Installing identically colored glass panels on the facades of both Idea Stores, Adjaye established a graphic element linking them, while also creating open and inviting thresholds, thin lines from the street that practically ask the community to come inside. Three more public-building commissions in London—including the Stephen Lawrence Center and the Bernie Grant Arts Center (2007; pages 121–27), both built with light-responsive metal cladding—were finished in the following years. Adjaye views the Bernie Grant project in particular as his first formal test for using the power of extruded metal to create a range of optical effects.

Shortly after the completion of Elektra House, in the firm's new studio space, Adjaye put materials at the forefront: assembled on a long bench, leading from the reception area to a conference room, was a full range of material samples. Referred to internally as the "Material Table," this system facilitated many of the uncommon material combinations that would become central, recurring elements in Adjaye's buildings, while also allowing the firm to never pigeonhole itself into a set style, feel, or aesthetic. "With the options laid out on the Material Table as the starting point," Adjaye has written, "we were interested in developing a material language that could engage with specific situations and [that], at a later stage, would connect one project with another. Our aim was to explore a diversity of systems that have common roots."[13] The Material Table became not just a tool for choosing the materials for a project, but also, by analyzing their physical and visual properties, a way of orchestrating a big-picture strategy across an array of projects.

In the late 1990s and 2000s, with the rise of various software-rendering programs, virtual reality technology, and simulation techniques, the study of physical material properties began to wane within architecture schools and studios,[14] but this was not the case at Adjaye Associates, which keeps material studies front and center. In her book *Material Transfers*, the architect Françoise Astorg Bollack notes that, among a certain cohort of contemporary firms in this new technological age, "the relationship between metaphor, materials, and craft is being tested and restated."[15] Adjaye's practice has risen to become among the foremost of this kind of testing and restating.

The Upper Room (1999–2002), an installation in collaboration with artist Chris Ofili, first installed at the Victoria Miro gallery in London and later shown at Tate Britain (pictured below), where it was added to the permanent collection.

"Material Table," as seen installed at the Aram Gallery in London, July 2011.

In the early 2000s, Adjaye saw the completion of two breakthrough projects that exemplify his approach to modulating climate and mediating light through material: Dirty House (2002) and Lost House (2004). The former, a squat, rough-textured, light-absorbing monolith in London's Shoreditch neighborhood, was built for the artists Sue Webster and Tim Noble. Embracing simple materials—concrete, brick, plaster, glass—the design establishes a sort of modern-day fortress, at once heavy in its broody, black-painted heft, and light, with its recessed flat white roof. The latter, a timber structure situated in the city's Kings Cross area and punctuated by three "vitrines," or courtyards, is what Adjaye calls "a meteorological or climatic observer." The landscape architect James Corner has described Le Corbusier's plan for Chandigarh (1951) in India and Lawrence Halprin's Sea Ranch (1963–98) in California as "inventively designed to optimize the physical environment as a creative and functioning organism: living, breathing, working, exchanging energy, and propagating new sets of effects."[16] Largely negotiating between outside and inside, Adjaye's work extends from and continues in this tradition, and could be described as such, too.

Adjaye's first completed project in the United States, a four-story building (2006) in Brooklyn's Fort Greene neighborhood for the studios of artists Lorna Simpson and James Casebere.

Around this time, Adjaye also won the commission to design the Museum of Contemporary Art Denver (2007; pages 220–29), a project that further elevated his profile and helped propel his work in the United States. (This followed his first project in America, a four-story, black-paneled structure in Brooklyn, completed in 2006, for the artists Lorna Simpson and James Casebere.) Constructed of continuously glazed walls—a tinted, sandblasted glass external wall, with an inner wall made of white translucent plastic—and skylights, the MCA Denver building effectively functions as a neighborhood lightbox. It is also what Adjaye (and the Smithsons) would define as a climate moderator, providing an airy atmosphere that allows for viewing and presenting art while integrating the world outside. In certain rooms, from certain vantages, one gets the feeling of nearly floating in space. A hanging installation by Teresita Fernández, composed of colored tubes in varying shades of pink and black, and positioned in the museum's central atrium from 2013 through 2014, provided the exact kind of alchemic reaction between art and architecture that Adjaye had intended with his design.

Teresita Fernández's *Night Writing* (2013), installed in the atrium of the Adjaye-designed Museum of Contemporary Art Denver (2007).

Throughout the 2000s, just as Adjaye had done in his RCA years, he continued to travel and engage in deep observation. From 2002 to 2006, he hosted BBC television and radio programs, for which he visited countries including Brazil, India, Japan, and Spain, and interviewed such architects as Charles Correa and Oscar Niemeyer. Starting in 2000, Adjaye also undertook an eleven-year research study of every capital city of Africa, the result of which became a London Design Museum exhibition and multi-volume book of photographs. The encyclopedic study was, on the whole, not just about African architecture and urbanism, but the alchemy of the continent—its incredible phenomenological mix of architecture, culture, geography, and climate. "Alchemy, in the context of Africa, is very normal," Adjaye says. "It's part of the way in which creativity operates. It seems unusual in the West, because it's not the normal way in which it happens—it's much more logical and organized [there]. Whereas, the notion of transformation, or transfiguration even, is a very African thing: you take something, and you transform it into another state, and then it becomes creatively admired."

Adjaye's travels throughout Africa led him to look especially closely at animism—the theory or belief that there's a spiritual essence or energy embedded in everything. What he came to realize was that, "to perceive form, you have to create the right combination of contrasts, and that there is no such thing as too much or too little—there's just combinations." Adjaye took note of the tactile nature and articulated facades of the continent's buildings and cityscapes, and particularly the effect that sunlight has on them. During his travels, he also gained a greater understanding of tropical modernism, or at least of its postwar African variations. He realized how, even with so many materials available to work with on the continent, most of the buildings actually employed very few. The architecture there tends to put an emphasis on tactile nature of the surfaces, an approach that reframes the very materials themselves.[17]

Nkron (2012), a private villa in Gomoa Fetteh, Ghana.

Hill House (2015) in Port of Spain, Trinidad and Tobago.

Soon enough, this deep engagement with and focus on Africa led to a stream of projects on the continent, beginning with his first building in 2012, the earth-pigmented, terra-cotta–colored concrete Nkron villa in Gomoa Fetteh, Ghana, for the diplomat Kofi Annan. Integrated into and extending out from the site's hilly topography, and comprising a cellular system of nine volumes, the two-story house represents a slight break in Adjaye's practice—from one that was primarily urban to one that began to explore landscape through, as he puts it, "perching and observing." The home is all about the extended view, in line with the Japanese principle of *shakkei*, or "borrowed scenery." The Specere Pavilion (2009) at Kielder National Park in Scotland, the Moscow School of Management SKOLKOVO campus (2010, pages 230–39) in Russia, and the white-tinted concrete Hill House (2015) embedded into a wooded hillside in Port of Spain, Trinidad, also contributed to this transition.

The next decade brought about a global expansion—one might even go so far as to call it an explosion—of the architect's practice, with a diverse portfolio of projects around the world, from the Gwangju River Reading Room (2013; pages 184–89) in South Korea, to the Piety Bridge and Wharf (2014; pages 128–33) in New Orleans, to the Alara concept store (2016) in Lagos, Nigeria. These projects allowed Adjaye to elaborate on his material palette, pushing his studies further and further with each job. With this came significant recognition: in 2015, Adjaye's work became the subject of a major retrospective exhibition at the Haus der Kunst in Munich and the Art Institute of Chicago, and in 2017 he was knighted by the late Queen Elizabeth II, as well as recognized as one of the hundred most influential people of the year by *Time* magazine.

Alara concept store (2016) in Lagos, Nigeria.

Hovering above all this was Adjaye's largest, most important commission to date: the career-defining Smithsonian National Museum of African American History and Culture (NMAAHC), completed in 2016. In 2015, describing his rapid trajectory—from Elektra House, to the MCA Denver, to SKOLKOVO, to the NMAAHC—Adjaye said, "There's a confidence that's been built. What's come out of it is that I'm now clear about what I want to do and how I want to do it." For Adjaye, the NMAAHC represented a new commitment to making large-scale public works, as well as a mature capability for achieving them. "In the beginning," he said, "[my practice] was much more intuitive, and now I'm able to articulate what the strategic decisions are and how the results are made."[18]

Situated adjacent to the Washington Monument, the NMAAHC literally and figuratively reflects on its specific five-acre site, as well as on its place in America and in the world. A steel-and-glass box, in fitting contrast with the Tennessee marble norm of the National Mall, the building is wrapped in a screen of bronze-painted aluminum. Formed into a three-tiered corona crown—a reference to a Yoruban sculpture—it features a lattice exterior based on ironworks fabricated by Black artisans in the American South. In a quiet, Souto de Moura–esque wink, its facade is pointed at the same 17.5-degree angle as the Washington Monument's capstone. Here, too, climate moderation is at play: inside the central atrium, dappled sunlight filters through, creating a warm, glowing effect.

At the NMAAHC, heading up the museum's escalators toward the upper-floor galleries, it is not surprising for someone to experience the kind of rare visceral sensation—an alchemic response, really—that one can have upon walking through or around truly extraordinary architecture. Whether stumbling upon Dirty House in East London, visiting an installation of the blackened timber Horizon Pavilion (2007; pages 157–65), or crossing Piety Bridge, this sort of reaction is frequently elicited from Adjaye's designs. All of these projects, while completely different—built years apart, located hundreds or thousands of miles away from each other, and in varying typologies and forms—still somehow achieve a singular feeling and phenomena.

Only occasionally in architecture, design, and art do the material conditions combine, in just the right way, to form an otherworldly confluence. In his 1958 book *The Poetics of Space*, the French philosopher Gaston Bachelard pinpoints it as "a sudden salience on the surface of the psyche."[19] The Swiss architect Jacques Herzog has described it as "the moment when materiality transcends into immateriality";[20] the Museum of Modern Art curator Paola Antonelli has termed it "mutational power."[21] The artist Thaddeus Mosley has defined it as "turning something natural into something alive."[22] A heightening of the senses occurs when multiple factors—materials, structure, and form; the surrounding environment; various climatic effects; and time—fuse together and embed themselves into one's psyche, creating deep memory and meaning. Through each project, with his alchemic vision, Adjaye seeks to achieve the salience of which Balechard writes.

In her book *Urban Alchemy*, the social psychiatrist Mindy Thompson Fullilove, unpacks what she calls the "visceral, never-to-be forgotten pleasure of place." One key way of archiving this sensation, she writes, is to make a mark on the cityscape: "The place outsiders *move through* can assert its claim to be a place outsiders may, and perhaps should, *go to*."[23] That's perhaps Adjaye's greatest skill as an architect. In sheer material wonder, his buildings pull people in, welcome delight, and create strong connections. His is a largely inclusive architecture, built for outsiders. "Becoming an urban alchemist," Fullilove writes, "begins with seeing the desires that are all around us and developing a faith that these can flow together to shape the spaces we share."[24] That's Adjaye, a creator of profound material and spatial relationships that physically, socially, and emotionally orient individuals and communities.

To a certain extent, Adjaye's approach could be viewed in parallel within the Japanese concept of *wabi-sabi*, or "the state of grace arrived at by a sober, modest, heartfelt intelligence," as defined by the artist and author Leonard Koren. Practically defining alchemy, Koren notes that *wabi-sabi* is shaped through "the invisible connective tissue that somehow binds the elements into a meaningful whole."[25] Through his various combinations of materials that are often irregular, intimate, unpretentious, earthy, and dark—all elements within Koren's overview of *wabi-sabi*—Adjaye's work aligns with much of the Japanese philosophy, though not necessarily in any direct or dogmatic way. His buildings serve as expressions for how he views, thinks about, and engages with materials and, by extension, the planet.

In this vein, Adjaye's work also connects with that of the Japanese-American artist and sculptor Isamu Noguchi. As with Noguchi's works, Adjaye's architecture has a poetic sensibility, a lightness of touch, a gracefulness, an ethereality, and a warmth. Adjaye and Noguchi share an appreciation for and an understanding of light and shadow, abstraction, and tactility. There is indeed a sculptural quality to much of Adjaye's architecture, one that's especially evident in his 130 William tower, a precast concrete rhomboidal structure that reaches upward toward the sky. It is an architectural form not dissimilar to Constantin Brâncuși's *Endless Column* sculpture, a motif that also had a strong influence on Noguchi (who, in 1927, had worked under Brâncuși in Paris).

Viewing his architecture within the vast sweep of human history and as part of a long, ongoing conversation across time, Adjaye thinks broadly and contextually. He understands that his work is very much of the now, but also that it is rooted in the far-off past, stemming from and growing out of ancient Greek and Roman practices, Japanese and African traditions, and twentieth-century Modernism, from Eileen Gray to Hassan Fathy. Praising the latter for his conceptual constructions, Adjaye describes the work of Fathy, a pioneering Egyptian architect who worked from the late 1930s through the early 1980s, as "the highest bar of radical architecture, in terms of being able to safely use the limits of material and the possibility of the earth right in front of you to create extraordinary dignity."

Adjaye does not shy away from sharing his kaleidoscopic list of influences, including Luis Barragán, for the spectral and chromatic effects of light on his concrete buildings; Louis Kahn, for his spiritual depth and painterly ability to harness light; and Carlo Scarpa, for his capacity to work within limits, igniting material investigation. And while he certainly pulls cues from these references, today Adjaye stands out for his own specific approach, which the late curator and critic Okwui Enwezor has described as "a distinctive contemporary 'Afropolitan' view."[26] Serving as a manifestation of his global perspective, shrewd urban-design know-how, East-meets-West ethos, and deep-seated Africanness, Adjaye's architecture combines traditional techniques and a human touch with modern technology and engineering. His radical, inside-Africa-out viewpoint negotiates new ways of operating in the world, with the aim of creating something magical.

Respecting the many levels of "place," Adjaye's buildings serve as dynamic reflections of their positions in the world. As with Kahn's and Frank Lloyd Wright's architecture, in his own work Adjaye takes what the historian John Lobell describes as "the Japanese position, feeling that each material—steel, concrete, brick, wood—has a will to express its nature."[27] Conscious meditations of space and material, Adjaye's buildings open up, unfold, and reveal themselves over time. Memory is at the core of his work: whether explicitly or not, each of his structures is a memorial in its own way, from Dirty House, to the NMAAHC, to Mole House (2019; pages 74–79) in London's Hackney neighborhood, to the Martyrs Memorial (expected to be completed in 2026) in Niamey, Niger. The materials Adjaye's uses, particularly in the very way he uses them, effectively become metaphorical mini-memorials, tactile expressions of where they came from.

Throughout his career, Adjaye has continued to create place-defining projects that function as local landmarks, elevating environments in heightened, often unexpected ways. At the McCarter Switching Station in Newark, he turned a utility structure from what would have likely become a neighborhood eyesore into an open-air art gallery and inviting public square. With The Webster concept shop (2020; pages 80–87) in Los Angeles, he brought a sensorial, highly crafted presence to an otherwise soulless retail strip. At the 1199 SEIU United Healthcare Workers East headquarters (2020; pages 88–93) in Manhattan, a Scarpa-esque staircase surprises and delights visitors upon entering; ceramic wall mosaics stop visitors in their tracks, inviting contemplation.

In 2019, following decades during which he was based primarily in London and New York, Adjaye moved to Accra, Ghana, with his family, a relocation that has expanded both his imagination and his work on the African continent. While he currently has projects underway all over the world—in countries including Australia, India, the UK, the US, and the United Arab Emirates—in recent years Adjaye has put a particular focus on building in Africa, landing several high-profile commissions there: the Thabo Mbeki Presidential Library in Johannesburg, the Edo Museum of West African Art in Nigeria, and the National Cathedral of Ghana in Accra among them. In the process, he has formed a particular interest in the construction of rammed-earth structures (see pages 253–77).

At its heart, Adjaye's architecture is about much more than just making evocative, tactile buildings and environments; it's about a particular rooted-in-the-earth philosophy. This special alchemy is what this book, organized around five material realms—Stone and Concrete, Metal, Wood, Glass, and Rammed Earth—seeks to define and unpack. For Adjaye, architecture provides an opportunity "to reach past what we see in ourselves, and to see something that unifies us as human beings." Literal and figurative connective tissue, Adjaye's buildings bind people and the planet. In his hands, materials make vast, cosmic connections.

A rendering of the Thabo Mbeki Presidential Library in Johannesburg, South Africa.

1
Juhani Pallasmaa, *The Eyes of the Skin: Architecture and the Senses* (2012), Wiley, 13.

2
Diane Ackerman, *An Alchemy of Mind* (2004), Scribner, 44.

3
Spencer Bailey, "Climate Moderator," *Surface*, 120, August 2015, 86.

4
Peter Allison, ed., *David Adjaye: Constructed Narratives* (2017), Lars Müller Publishers, 91.

5
Spencer Bailey, "Buildings Have Feelings Too," *Town & Country*, April 2019, 37.

6
Nathaniel Coleman, *Materials and Meaning in Architecture: Essays on the Bodily Experience of Buildings*, Bloomsbury (2020), 74.

7
Marc McQuade, ed., *David Adjaye: Authoring* (2012), Lars Müller Publishers, 108–9.

8
Diane Solway, "Where In The World Is David Adjaye?," *W*, March 1, 2011.

9
Calvin Tomkins, "A Sense of Place," *The New Yorker*, September 23, 2013.

10
Virginia Ponciroli, ed., *Katsura Imperial Villa* (2013), Phaidon Press, 10.

11
McQuade, *David Adjaye: Authoring*, 1.

12
Peter Allison, ed., *David Adjaye: Geographies* (2015), Franz Schneider Braken GmbH + Co KG, 41.

13
Allison, ed., *David Adjaye: Constructed Narratives*, 94.

14
Toshiko Mori, ed., *Immaterial/ Ultramaterial*, XIII.

15
Françoise Astorg Bollack, *Material Transfers: Metaphor, Craft, and Place in Contemporary Architecture* (2020), Monacelli Press, 8.

16
Silvia Benedito, *Atmosphere Anatomies: On Design, Weather, and Sensation* (2021), Lars Müller Publishers, 348.

17
Okwui Enwezor and Zoe Ryan, eds. *David Ajdaye: Form, Heft, Material* (2015), Yale University Press, The Art Institute of Chicago, Haus der Kunst, 71.

18
Bailey, "Climate Moderator," *Surface*, 80.

19
Gaston Bachelard, *The Poetics of Space* (2014 [1958]), Penguin Books, 1.

20
Mori, ed., *Immaterial/Ultramaterial*, 81.

21
Paola Antonelli, *Mutant Materials in Contemporary Design* (1995), The Museum of Modern Art, 9.

22
Brett Litmann, "Animated Abstractions," *Thaddeus Moseley* (2020), Karma, 42.

23
Mindy Thompson Fullilove, *Urban Alchemy: Restorying Joy in America's Sorted-Out Cities* (2013), New Village Press, 125.

24
Fullilove, *Urban Alchemy*, 303.

25
Leonard Koren, *Wabi-Sabi for Artists, Designers, Poets & Philosophers*, Imperfect Publishing, 62–72.

26
Okwui Enwezor and Zoe Ryan, eds. *David Adjaye: Form, Heft, Material*, 16.

27
John Lobell, *Louis Kahn: Architecture as Philosophy* (2020), Monacelli Press, 42.

Stone and Concrete

Concrete Garden
London, UK, 2001

Dirty House
London, UK, 2002

Nanjing House
Nanjing, CN, 2012

Sugar Hill Mixed-Use Development
New York, NY, US, 2015

McCarter Switching Station
Newark, NJ, US, 2018

Ruby City
San Antonio, TX, US, 2019

Mole House
London, UK, 2019

The Webster
Los Angeles, CA, US, 2020

199 SEIU United Healthcare Workers East
New York, NY, US, 2020

130 William
New York, NY, US, 2021

Winter Park Library
Winter Park, FL, US, 2021

Abrahamic Family House
Abu Dhabi, UAE, 2023

More than any other materials in David Adjaye's architectural arsenal (other than, perhaps, rammed earth), stone and concrete stand out as the most evocative—hefty geologic connection points between ancient times and modern. Adjaye's stone and concrete buildings intimately reflect on the time it took to create each structure, whether over millions of years, as with the stacked stones of Nanjing House (2012) in China, or via swift pours, in the case of the pink-hued concrete of The Webster (2020) in Los Angeles. Stone and concrete are "our earliest understanding of what architecture can be in the world," Adjaye says, "from the pyramids, right through to the Roman aqueducts, through to the Pantheon, through to wherever we are now." This across-time groundedness and astute sense of storytelling runs through Adjaye's work, from one of his earliest projects, the intimate Concrete Garden (2001) in London, to the sculptural 130 William skyscraper (2021) in downtown Manhattan.

Taking the long view, Adjaye uses stone and concrete, in part, for their enduring, long-lasting qualities—as a way of thinking big-picture architecturally. "If everything disappeared," he asks, "what would be left? These would be fragments for archeologists to understand our time." In many ways, Adjaye's concrete and stone structures are made, from the start, to be relics and memorials, temporal testaments to human existence. Accepting—and even honoring—the interim nature inherent in architecture, Adjaye understands with acuity that each building will have its own life, existing in its own distinct way, responding to and evolving with the climate, culture, and society around it. With great sensitivity, Adjaye thinks about the materials he uses as an ecological energy force, one that's taken from the earth, and which in turn directly impacts and affects those who come in contact with it, and that may one day return into the ground. His stone and concrete structures—highly tactile showcases of frozen time—are perhaps the most potent forms of this thinking.

Adjaye describes concrete in particular as "intoxicating," and notes that he does not use it lightly. He understands and acknowledges the carbon-intensive nature of the material, but also sees that, when applied with great care through high-quality construction, it can stand the test of time, redefining notions of what might be called sustainable. Playing with various tonalities and textures, Adjaye molds concrete—whether poured in place on site or precast in a factory, whether black-pigmented or red-hued—into bold forms, creating what he describes as a "psychological density." Each resulting space becomes an emotional refuge, perhaps most notably experienced in his Sugar Hill mixed-use development (2015) in Harlem, New York City, because of that particular project's ability, through a heightened material engagement, to give dignity to—and elevate the lives of—its residents and neighborhood. The thirteen-story textured slab building, perched on the edge of 155th Street and St. Nicholas Avenue, comprises a precast black concrete facade with a custom rose-patterned form-liner, exuding a profound sense of physical, bodily strength. Similarly, with the McCarter Switching Station (2018) in Newark, New Jersey, Adjaye created a space that brings material weight, functional utility, and artistic expression to a low-income neighborhood, positing a future in which a city's "back-of-house" architecture can be celebrated and brought to the front. Powerful in their tactile qualities, moody and sometimes broody in their heft, arresting in their detail, and evocative through their engagement with light, Adjaye's stone and concrete structures—monumental regardless of scale—serve as deeply grounded touchstones that connect people and the planet through space and time.

Concrete Garden
London, UK, 2001

Concrete Garden is a little-known but decidedly definitive project within Adjaye's oeuvre—particularly when it comes to his firm's material palette. Built into the backyard of the south London home of a writer-editor-urbanist couple and located in the city's Dulwich neighborhood, Concrete Garden plays with the concept of an outdoor room, one intended to relieve its occupants of any need for gardening. For Adjaye, it was a rare open-ended commission: the opportunity to create an alternative built world—more or less a tabula rasa. The project would serve as an important early test around the power of how a material can emotionally shift perception.

A humble outdoor terrace made of reddish-brown pigmented concrete, framed by a continuous 7-foot-high (2.2-meter) wall—the maximum height allowed without requiring planning permission—the project was inspired in part by traditional Japanese architecture (in which certain spaces can be seen, but not entered), as well as by the red-earth adobe villages of sub-Saharan Africa. A celebration of emptiness and void, the space draws the eye to the material, color, and textural presence of the concrete, and also brings attention to the neighboring buildings, treetops, and chimneys, and to the sky above. In its spareness, it serves as a slate on which to bear witness to various atmospheric shifts and sensations, and seasonal and temporal conditions.

To create the color of the concrete, Adjaye added rust. The vermilion hue, which in sunlight becomes more bright and colorful and at night becomes subdued and recessive, extends to the Nkron private villa in Gomoa Fetteh, Ghana, built just over a decade later, in 2012, as well as to the Ruby City art center (2019; page 64) in San Antonio, Texas; to The Webster (2020; page 80) in Los Angeles; and into the firm's more recent rammed-earth projects (pages 250–73). Rounding out the sculptural design are benches and a bike shed, all made in this same material and a color that would become Adjaye's signature.

Top: Conceived as an earth-like enclosure, the red-hued concrete wall extends the perimeter of this "outdoor room," creating an intimate setting within the surrounding cityscape. *Bottom*: A material and structural counterpoint to the brick homes that define London's Dulwich neighborhood, the space frames contrasting views back to the brickwork.

In a circadian duet with sunlight, the textural pattern of the rust-tinted concrete appears brighter during the day and becomes a stage for ever-shifting shadows.

The heft of the concrete walls is balanced by the objects placed within it—in this case, seating configurations and floating planters.

At seven feet in height, the wall cultivates a void-like space that directs the eye up toward the sky and surrounding chimneys and rooflines.

Dirty House
London, UK, 2002

Dirty House marked the beginning of Adjaye's exploration of the "house within a house" concept. It is a case study for the architect's "recycling, reconfiguring, rebuilding" approach, which remains a central tenet of his practice. Building a new structure inside the walls of an old furniture factory in London's Shoreditch neighborhood—walls that required extensive repairs—Adjaye created both a home and a beacon. Dirty House's textured facade of brick and concrete testifies to many built histories, while also establishing something entirely novel.

Most notable is the home's brooding color itself, a deep, dark brown-purple that, depending on weather conditions, can appear black, highlighting its myriad material stories. To choose the hue and determine the building's look and feel even before construction, Adjaye and his team used computer-imaging software, relatively nascent at the time, to create precise color studies. In calling the house "dirty" and applying anti-graffiti paint, and in shaping its fortress-like form, Adjaye allowed the monolithic structure to function as a subtle architectural taunt and provocation. Rough and uneven, its shell carries a profound presence that absorbs light and atmosphere, as well as its physical surroundings. In its toned-down darkness, Dirty House's skin stands out from the neighboring buildings and, because of this, becomes light. Its cuboid form, heft, and materiality command attention, beckoning passersby to stop, look, and think. Its tinted reflective windows, too, offer a cheeky nod to the area's past as a red-light district, and to the vanity and voyeurism inherent in a rapidly changing neighborhood.

Inside, Adjaye gutted the interior to create a pair of the ground-floor studios (the clients were an artist couple, Sue Webster and Tim Noble), protected behind a thick exterior and mirrored glass. A promontory-like penthouse apartment caps the upper floor, cantilevered above and surrounded by a terrace parapet. To support the new structure and reinforce the existing building, Adjaye inserted steel columns on the inside face of the external walls; an additional layer of thermal insulation was added as well, fortifying the facade and creating deep window recesses on the second floor. At night, the top level's illuminated open-plan loft practically turns the entire structure into a giant lamp.

Top: The structure's monolithic form and black color form a provocative presence from the sidewalk. *Bottom:* The dark brick exterior walls, punctured with tinted window bays, contrast the lightness of the white cantilevered roof.

A high interior ceiling forms an atrium-like space, with light cascading down the white walls. The thick interior walls, layered for thermal insulation, form deep-set windows that artfully bring in natural light.

Left: The upper level is surrounded by a terrace parapet, with floor-to-ceiling windows and a central ceiling skylight. *Right*: The terrace, with views of the surrounding neighborhood.

Nanjing House
Nanjing, CN, 2012

To approach the design of Nanjing House, part of the Sifang Art Museum, Adjaye considered the mountainous region's topography and climate, and chose stone, specifically slate, as a medium with which to engage with the memory and layering of the city. Creating a kind of "hidden architecture," Adjaye constructed a high-walled, rectangular structure made of stacked off-cut stones, sourced from remainder pieces found at a nearby quarry. A result of the architect's intentional way of turning discards into something vibrant, purposeful, and new, the home and its textured facade serve as a deep-time testament to—and honoring of—the region, nodding to the past while remaining contemporary in feeling.

Built in Laoshan National Forest Park, across the Yangtze River from downtown Nanjing, the elevated, five-bedroom villa is one of a showcase of structures there by twenty-four architectural practices commissioned for the China International Practical Exhibition of Architecture. Inspired by parallel pedestrian lanes in traditional Asian city-making—forms now largely lost to rapid industrialization, urbanization, and sprawl—Adjaye created a weighty, bunkerlike design that, despite the bulk and heft of the stone, appears to practically levitate. In form and feeling, it is not entirely unlike the playful, ethereal homes of the Portuguese architect Eduardo Souto de Moura, under whom Adjaye once apprenticed.

Arranged in the form of a 196-foot-high (60-meter) horizontal box, surrounded by a wooded ravine on one side and a bamboo thicket on the other, the monolithic building frames extended views out from both of its ends. Inside, swooping, rounded walls and ceilings made of concrete are combined with timber flooring and stairs, creating an interplay between light and dark; mirror-finished stainless steel further accents the interior. Also punctuating the rooms are irregularly spaced, deep-recessed window apertures, a series of skylights, and several rectangular glazed openings on the floor. Throughout, the space unfolds, compresses, expands, and releases, resulting in a strong sense of resonance.

Slightly raised above the ground in a dramatic oblong form, the house features a facade clad with locally sourced slate off-cuts.

Top: Planes of concrete, bamboo, and stone are punctuated by openings that frame views of the landscape. *Bottom*: A warm wood staircase intersects with the curved concrete ceiling.

A vibrant play of light and shadow, created by a series of skylights and horizontal windows, elevates the concrete interior.

Left: A subtle entryway, cut into the center of the structure, features steps that lead to a front door. *Right*: A small square aperture in the stacked slate facade frames a view out to the surroundings, while also allowing light to animate the interior.

At night, lighting underneath the home visually "lifts" the monolithic stone form, with a large window at one end giving off a soft glow from within. *Following spread*: The structure's facade is interrupted by an irregular pattern of deep-set windows.

Sugar Hill Mixed-Use Development
New York, NY, US, 2015

Dramatically planted on the crest of the Coogan's Bluff promontory, at 155th Street and St. Nicholas Avenue in Harlem, the black, precast concrete–clad Sugar Hill mixed-use development, so named after its neighborhood, serves as a bold, brooding architectural signal. A built form of equity, community revitalization, and social currency, and a celebratory mash-up of the area's Black and African American history and culture, the monolithic structure is an acknowledgment of the absence of Black spaces within New York City's built environment, creating what Adjaye calls a "culture register."

Developed by the local nonprofit Broadway Housing Communities (BHC) and built on a foundation of family planning and childcare, the 171,085-square-foot (15,894-square-meter) tower features a ground-floor education center for young children, with eight classrooms walled with full-height glazing, and two private courtyards; below it is a light-filled children's museum. Above, spread over thirteen stories, are 124 timber-floored units, ranging from studios to three-bedroom apartments. Occupying the ninth-floor setback level, atop the building's 76-foot (26-meter) base, where a cantilever juts out, are a community room, BHC offices, and a terrace (other terraces are located on the second and third floors, as well as on the roof).

Carefully contextualized yet forming a striking silhouette, the building is adorned in an abstracted rose relief, for ornamental effect, that references nearby brownstones and cornices and pays tribute to the area's designation as the Heritage Rose District. For Adjaye, the motif and textured slab facade—embedded with recycled glass, to sparkle in the sunlight—carry a meaning that goes even deeper: the idea of Black fragility, of visibility and invisibility, of being precariously perched. The building could itself be viewed as a flower, proudly growing from the site's urban framework. Extending out of the language of early-career London projects, such as Elektra House (1999) and Dirty House (2002; page 34), its design also subtly references a series of nearby Gothic revival row houses, in the form of six staggered bays running along its north and south facades. Taken as a whole, through its distinctive combination of form, function, and materiality, Sugar Hill manifests the memory of the area and carves necessary new meaning into it.

The twelve-story structure features a dramatic cantilever that forms a highly recognizable neighborhood beacon.

Top: Paying tribute to the rich cultural history of Harlem, the precast cladding system unifies the building's exterior with an embossed rose pattern. *Bottom*: The precast concrete facade is punctuated with square windows.

In a playful repetition, six staggered bays add a high level of craft and detail to the monumental structure, while also nodding to surrounding row houses (see page 54). *Following spread*: An expansive view of the bays.

Top: A ninth-floor terrace provides sweeping vistas of the surrounding neighborhood.
Bottom: A ground-floor internal courtyard, connected to the building's childhood education center and museum.

Solid white interior walls reflect light deep into a central hallway and eight classrooms. *Following spread*: The cladding echoes the intricate Gothic Revival stone masonry visible in the bays of the neighboring row houses.

906 ST. NICHOLAS
GOURMET DELI & GROCERY
DELI
LUNCH
FREE DELIVERY
MANHATTAN RADIO
TWO WAY RADIOS
906
W 155 St

McCarter Switching Station Newark, NJ, US, 2018

Following Hurricane Sandy in 2012—which had a devastating impact on Newark and left around nine out of ten of the city's residents without power—the energy company PSEG set out to upgrade its infrastructure across the city. A core part of its plans included building a new switching station in the city's Fairmount Heights neighborhood. The project was not without controversy: there were protests at packed community meetings, with neighbors fearing an unsightly facility wedged into the middle of the surrounding residential streetscape. (Built on once-contaminated land, the four-and-a-half-acre lot previously contained a church and a scissors factory.) In a true collaboration, involving public and private entities and the local community, Adjaye established a sensitive design solution to provide both electrical infrastructure and help meet various neighborhood needs—economic, educational, recreational, and social.

Reconceptualized into a surprisingly serene 174,000-square-foot (16,165-square-meter) site of utility and culture, the McCarter Switching Station turns what would otherwise have been a neighborhood eyesore into a sweeping space of civic pride and an expansive, open-air art gallery that also happens to serve its necessary electrical-grid function. Original works by fourteen artists—including Xenobia Bailey, Willie Cole, Kevin Darmanie, Gladys Barker Grauer, Otto Neals, and Kevin Sampson—line an "art wall," made of curved, perforated aluminum and corrugated red precast concrete, that stretches 1,790 feet (545 meters) around the block, enclosing the substation. Most of the works are mounted high up on the 30-foot-tall (9.1-meter) walls, positioned in custom-cut niches. Landscaped green spaces surround its base along the perimeter, spanning about 10 feet (3 meters) in width.

Forming a central, symmetrically arranged *agora*, or public square, are fifty-two columned concrete canopies, each 24 feet (7.3 meters) in height, that serve to create a protective overhead cover. Allowing for market and community events to take place there, the beams also provide structural support for an overhead installation by the artist Lisa Soto. A pedestrian passageway along the building's north side provides access to the square from both east and west, maintaining a sense of openness.

Monumental concrete canopies reframe this civic infrastructure as a community space.

The earth-colored colonnade creates a distinct sense of place and connection to nature within an urban landscape.

Reveals between the elegantly arranged, 24-foot-high canopies frame views of the sky. From certain vantages, the covers of the canopies appear dynamic and weightless, almost as if in flight.

Convergence, an overhead, gridded art installation by Caribbean-American artist Lisa Soto suspends mirrored steel forms between the fifty-two columns.

Niches for permanent art installations are embedded into a vertical screen of curved perforated aluminum and corrugated precast concrete. *Following spread*: The colonnaded *agora*, or public square, allows for gatherings and community events.

Ruby City
San Antonio, TX, US, 2019

Months before her death from cancer in 2007, the artist, collector, and philanthropist Linda Pace drew a vision of a hilltop complex with palatial crystalline towers made of rubies—her version of an art-park Oz. She then tapped Adjaye, whom she had met through the British artist and filmmaker Isaac Julien, a mutual friend, to translate it into his own built creation. The agreement between Pace and Adjaye stipulated a ruby-colored building in which to present the 900-work collection of her foundation's art center. The resulting two-story, 14,000-square-foot (1,300-square-meter) structure, twelve years in the making, boldly takes cues from the region's Spanish Missions and the city's architectural heritage, as well as from the site's surrounding industrial landscape. For Adjaye, its angular, fortresslike form was, in part, a way to aggregate and distort the neighboring warehouses into something extraordinary and entirely new. Central to a campus plan, the building joins an adjacent one-acre public memorial park honoring Pace's son and an additional nearby exhibition space.

Made of red precast concrete, fabricated in Mexico City and encrusted with shards of red recycled glass that sparkle in the Texas sun, the exterior features a polished finish the first 10 feet (3 meters) up and, above that, an exposed, rough-textured wall. Around twenty studies were undertaken to imbue the concrete in exactly the right shade of red, a color not only emblematic of Pace's vision, but also of the region's clay-filled earth. The material appears throughout: in custom curbside bollards and benches, across the exterior entry courtyard, and in the interior lobby floor. Crowning the building are two "lanterns" that bring natural light down into the galleries and contribute further toward creating the setting's luminous, prismatic glow; a shaded side window punctuates the structure, giving it a sculptural quality.

At the entrance, the building cantilevers out, offering a shaded porch and a subtle architectural wave to passersby. Inside, on the ground floor, the reception area features a large concrete desk designed by Adjaye and a steep staircase leading up to the exhibition spaces; staff offices and a conference room look out at the sculpture garden. On the second floor, 10,000 square feet (925 meters) of exhibition space is divided into three large galleries, two of which are high-ceilinged and naturally lit from above by clerestory windows covered with expanded metal mesh. In its own quiet way, Ruby City is both a space for art and a memorial—a meaningful tribute to the woman who dreamed it up.

The large structure cantilevers over the entry plaza, inviting visitors into a shaded glass porch.

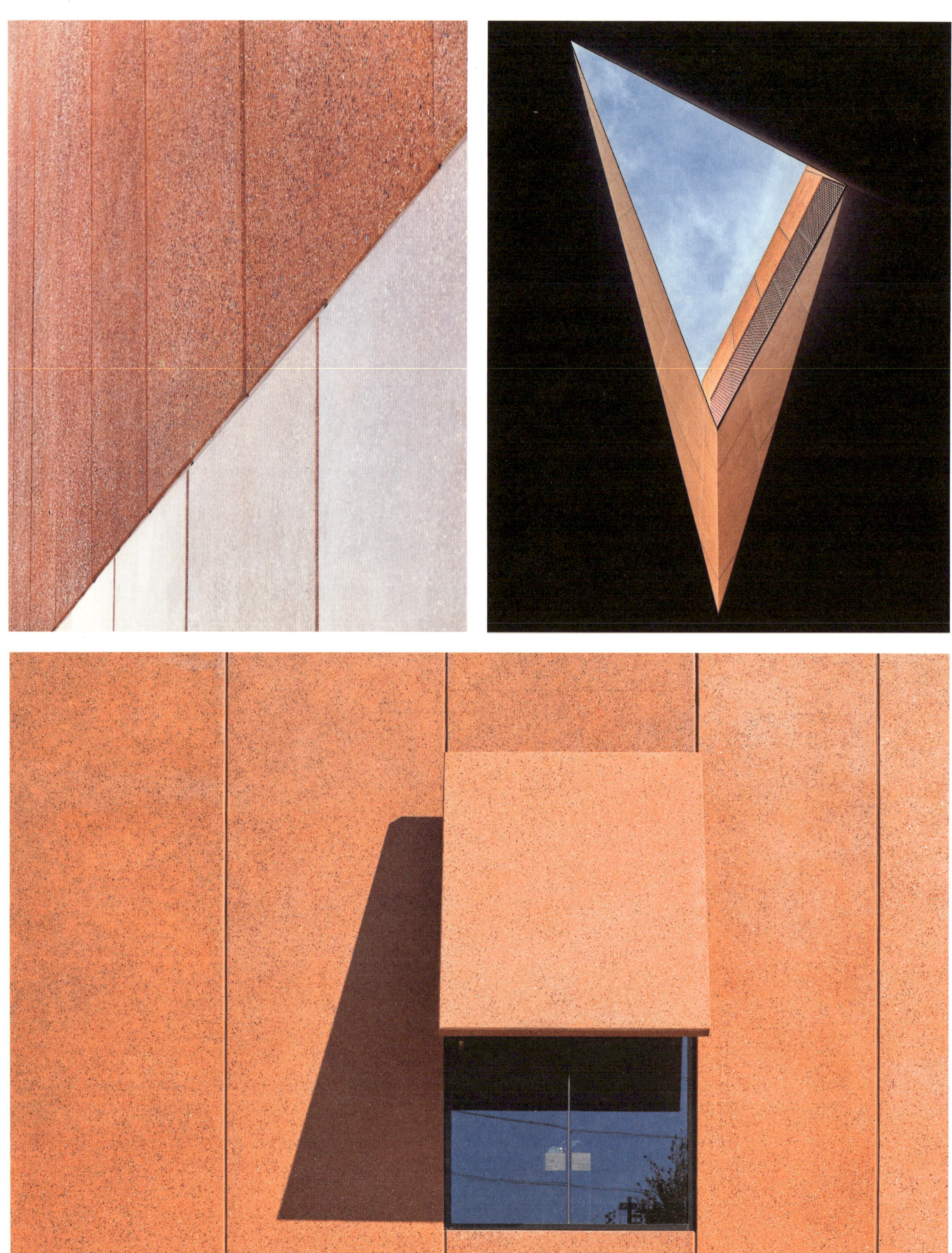

The facade dissolves through the introduction of textural shifts, color grades, and apertures that punctuate the building.

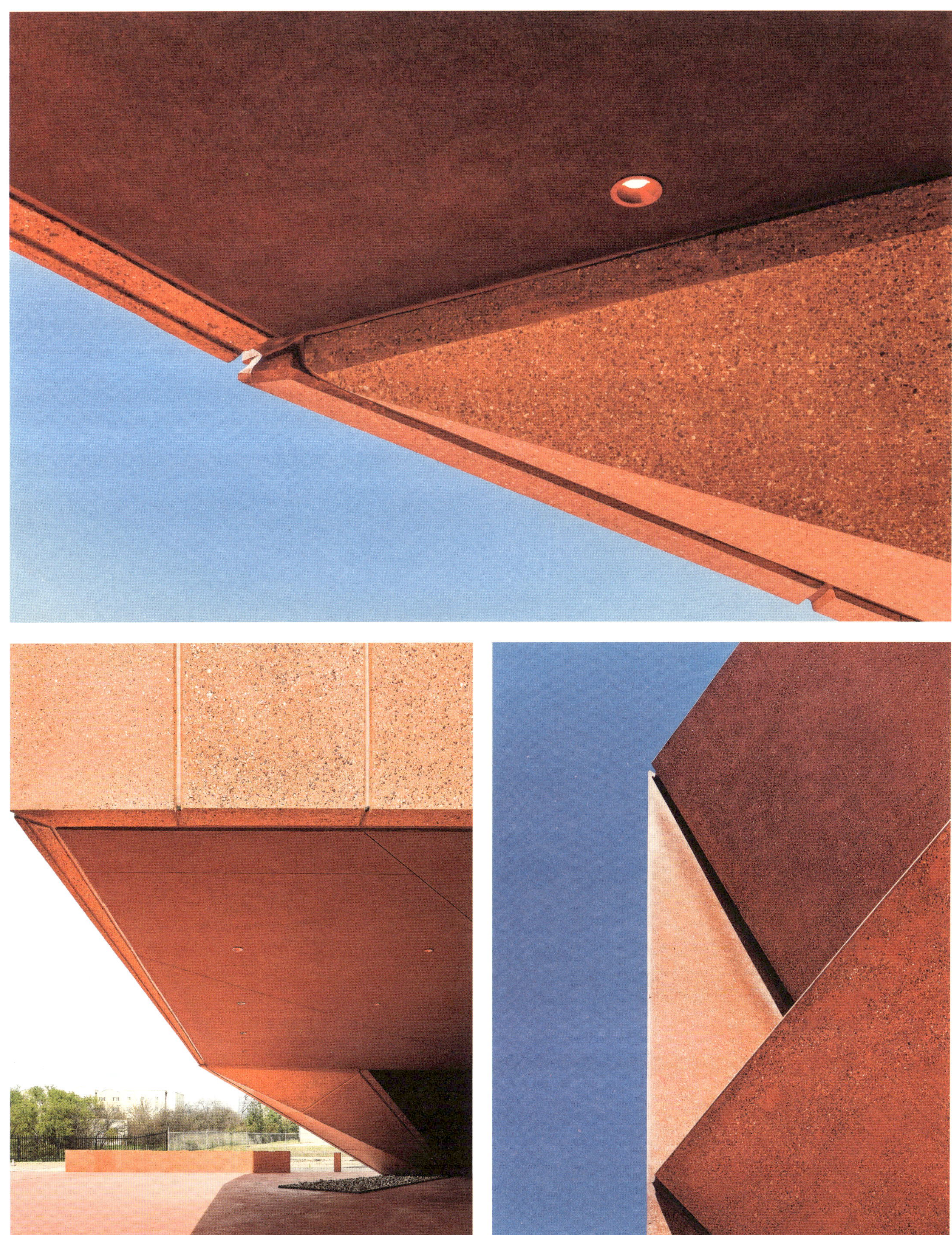

Rich, red precast concrete, composed with recycled glass shards, envelops the building's sculptural form, forming a glinting, jewel-like surface.

The sloping, high-ceilinged roofline opens up the gallery space inside, with natural light from above washing the gallery below.

Light, airy interior galleries are punctuated by a large "eyelid" window overlooking the sculpture garden. *Following spread*: The building appears as if an angular, sculpted, sparkling rock.

RUBY

Glass windows on the facade above the building's main entrance reflect the San Antonio sky during the day.

The first ten vertical feet of the building's exterior has a polished finish, inviting passersby to touch the concrete. Above, the concrete is rough, sharp, and encrusted with two hues of red glass.

Mole House
London, UK, 2019

Located in the East London suburb of De Beauvoir Town, Mole House extends from an unusual, decidedly ragtag history: William Lyttle, the property's previous owner, occupied the site from the early 1960s until 2006. Known locally as "Mole Man," over the years he dug a series of tunnels underneath the Victorian villa, breaking through its foundations and, to hold it up, constructing makeshift pillars out of shuttered concrete. (He also built various enclosures, terraces, staircases, and even an outdoor pool and garden.) Eventually, the local council, the London Borough of Hackney, evicted Lyttle, citing the building as structurally compromised. Purchasing the derelict property in 2012—by then, its roof had caved in—the artist Sue Webster, who had first commissioned Adjaye for her previous home, Dirty House (2002; page 34), had a specific vision for its restoration and revitalization: to respect the "as-found" character of the place, including Lyttle's various interventions, while also designing a practical space in which to live and work.

Approaching the project in an archeological and, to a point, conservational way, Adjaye embraced the eclectic property's many layers: the original brick structure; Lyttle's handmade concrete insertions and counter-forms, often filled with pipes and waste; and the two thousand tons of aerated concrete that the council had filled the tunnels with. Inside, Adjaye gutted the interior and created three levels, with a two-bedroom, skylit residential space on the top two floors and an art studio on the ground floor. A central cross-shaped concrete organizing device divides the floors and supports the structure, bringing together concrete ceilings, a cantilevered concrete staircase, and pine floors. Douglas fir joinery is applied throughout.

Outside, past a green metal gate on a sharp-pointed corner between two roads, a concrete staircase leads down into a sunken garden with a terrace overlooking it. To the south of the house, a parking space is supported on an existing concrete vault. The building's stucco and brick facade, for the most part untouched, features bay windows (the street-facing ones covered in mirrored vinyl) that were rebuilt in steel and cast concrete. More than fifteen thousand reclaimed bricks encase the property, with timber posts used for the front gate and as parking fencing; original masonry was also retained. A sleek steel band caps the building, with a slate-covered roof topping it off.

Layers of the site's historical foundation were revealed through a careful and methodical process of excavation, as seen from this internal courtyard.

Left: Light illuminates the staircase leading up out of (or down into) the home's sunken "archeological" garden. *Right*: A preserved "ruin" from the original building, with a drainage pipe sticking out.

The perimeter wall of the home's triangular plot reflects the original masonry, with fifteen thousand reclaimed London bricks used to supplant areas of excess damage. *Following spread*: A sense of temporal entanglement arises out of the blend of old and new, renovation and restoration, material choices and urban histories.

The Webster
Los Angeles, CA, US, 2020

For the Los Angeles outpost of the fashion boutique The Webster, Adjaye's first project in California, the architect and client sought to invert both the notion of a retail space and the project site itself. Anchoring the base of the eight-story Los Angeles Beverly Center, at the intersection of San Vicente and Beverly Boulevards—and wedged into and projecting out of it—the 11,000-square-foot (1,020-square-meter) squat, sculptural structure exudes a pronounced presence, providing both a sensory shopping experience and an inviting public square. Referencing and reimagining the shell of the existing building, while also harking back to the material palette of one of his earliest projects, Concrete Garden (2001; page 29) in London, Adjaye designed a curvy, cantilevered facade and columnless portico in pink-dyed concrete that juts out and firmly establishes a communal atmosphere. The landmark-like meeting point features a digital art wall, intentionally high-resolution horizontally and low-resolution vertically, and a water fountain.

A study in luminosity and a subtle nod to the work of the Mexican architect Luis Barragán, The Webster elegantly merges toughness and softness through light, shadow, and color. Three sheets of curved glass at the entrance offer a panoramic view outside and reveal a landscape of sinuous forms inside: concrete columns; cylindrical concrete display plinths protruding from the walls, underneath artificially lit lightwells; a cantilevered concrete reception desk; and leather-upholstered concrete benches. A range of concrete—precast, glass-fiber reinforced, and cast in place, with a variety of finishes—primarily makes up the space. Outside, a salt additive was used on the upper section of the facade to create a perforated texture; inside, terrazzo floors feature a black cherry aggregate, with chips of limestone, marble, and granite. The upper walls and ceiling, in the same pinkish-red pigment as the concrete, are made of textured industrial plaster. Brass railings and vintage floral wall coverings from the personal collection of the client, Laure Hériard Dubreuil, round out the space.

Playing with the boundaries between outside and inside, street and shop, The Webster is a meditation on the Beverly Center's history, the specific site itself, and the city of Los Angeles and state of California. Despite the challenges of the location on which it sits and the surrounding urban sprawl, the building, in its bold juxtaposition, forms a strong sense of place and a welcome, textural counterpoint within the LA cityscape.

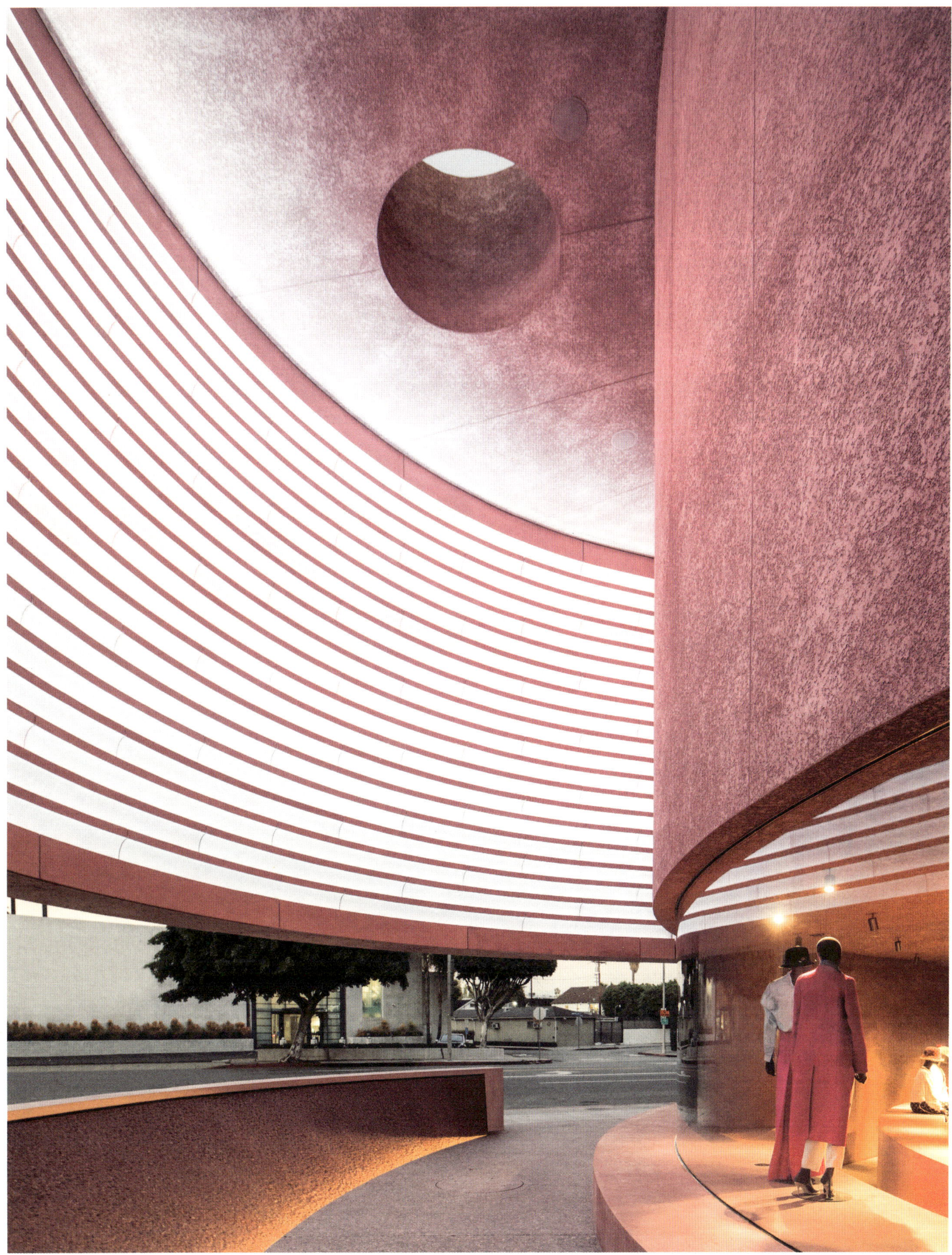

The Webster's entryway features a soft, curving media display wall; an ethereal oculus; and bench seating along the window display, becoming a serene public square. *Following spread*: From outside, there's a sculpted, almost cave-like quality to the light-filled structure.

THE WEBSTER

A range of materials and finishes compose the exterior palette. Terrazzo floors feature a black cherry stone aggregate, with chips of limestone, marble, and granite. The pinkish-red pigment of the concrete base is extended to the upper walls and treated with a salt additive to create a perforated texture.

The material palette of the exterior spills into the interior. Sculptural cast-in-place concrete columns and teardrop-shaped plinths form a series of vignettes for merchandise displays. *Following spread*: The store's cantilevered concrete dramatically juts out from the Beverly Center.

157
WEBSTER VALET PARKING

1199 SEIU United Healthcare Workers East
New York, NY, US, 2020

When 1199 SEIU, the largest health-care union in the United States (founded in 1932), decided to move its Midtown Manhattan headquarters several blocks, to better accommodate its growing membership, it selected Adjaye to shape its 16,500 square feet (1,500 square meters) of public member areas, including a lobby, lounges, and meeting rooms, as well as an art gallery and a library. Translating the social justice ethos of the organization into soaring interior architecture across four floors, Adjaye also sought to literally bring a part of the previous SEIU structure to the new: a monumental 1970 Anton Refregier mosaic mural. Depicting the union's members, the artwork features a central panel with a quote from social reformer Frederick Douglass: "If there is no struggle, there can be no progress."

Adjaye and his team soon realized, however, that deinstalling and relocating the Refregier mural would prove impossible without damaging it. With the union, they instead decided to create a reproduction, also fitting it within certain constraints of the new space. Working with a mosaic artist, the team made a faithfully updated mural that beckons visitors up into the headquarters. Alongside it, an evocative, highly crafted staircase, reminiscent of the work of Carlo Scarpa, encourages even greater architectural engagement. Further up, along the same wall as the mural, is a three-story-high effigy of the Rev. Dr. Martin Luther King Jr., with select quotes, in brass, from a speech he once gave to the SEIU. (King addressed the union, referring to himself as a "fellow 1199-er," just six weeks before his assassination, on April 4, 1968.)

Throughout the upper floors, the walls are lined with black-and-white ceramic photo tileworks, hand-pressed by the Cerámica Suro tile factory in Guadalajara, Mexico, and arranged in two-by-two-inch grids. Created from eighty or so images that Adjaye selected from the SEIU archive, the tiles showcase an array of important figures, from Barack Obama to Jesse Jackson, as well as highlight labor-rights milestones and various historic moments, including Vietnam War protests and AIDS activism. Maintaining a quiet material palette, Adjaye inserted touches of brass and polished black marble that, when paired with the ceramic tiles, manage to add both weight and lightness. Terrazzo and travertine floors complement with the glass-fiber-reinforced concrete panels that make up the structural columns and swooping barrel vaults that run along the ceilings. All together, the materials establish an intimate atmosphere—one far more evocative of a museum than an office.

Ceramic tile murals, barrel-vaulted ceilings made from glass fiber reinforced gypsum cement, concrete columns, and terrazzo flooring culminate in an immersive visitor experience.

Archival murals displaying SEIU's history (an image featuring Jesse Jackson is shown at right) celebrate key milestones of the organization.

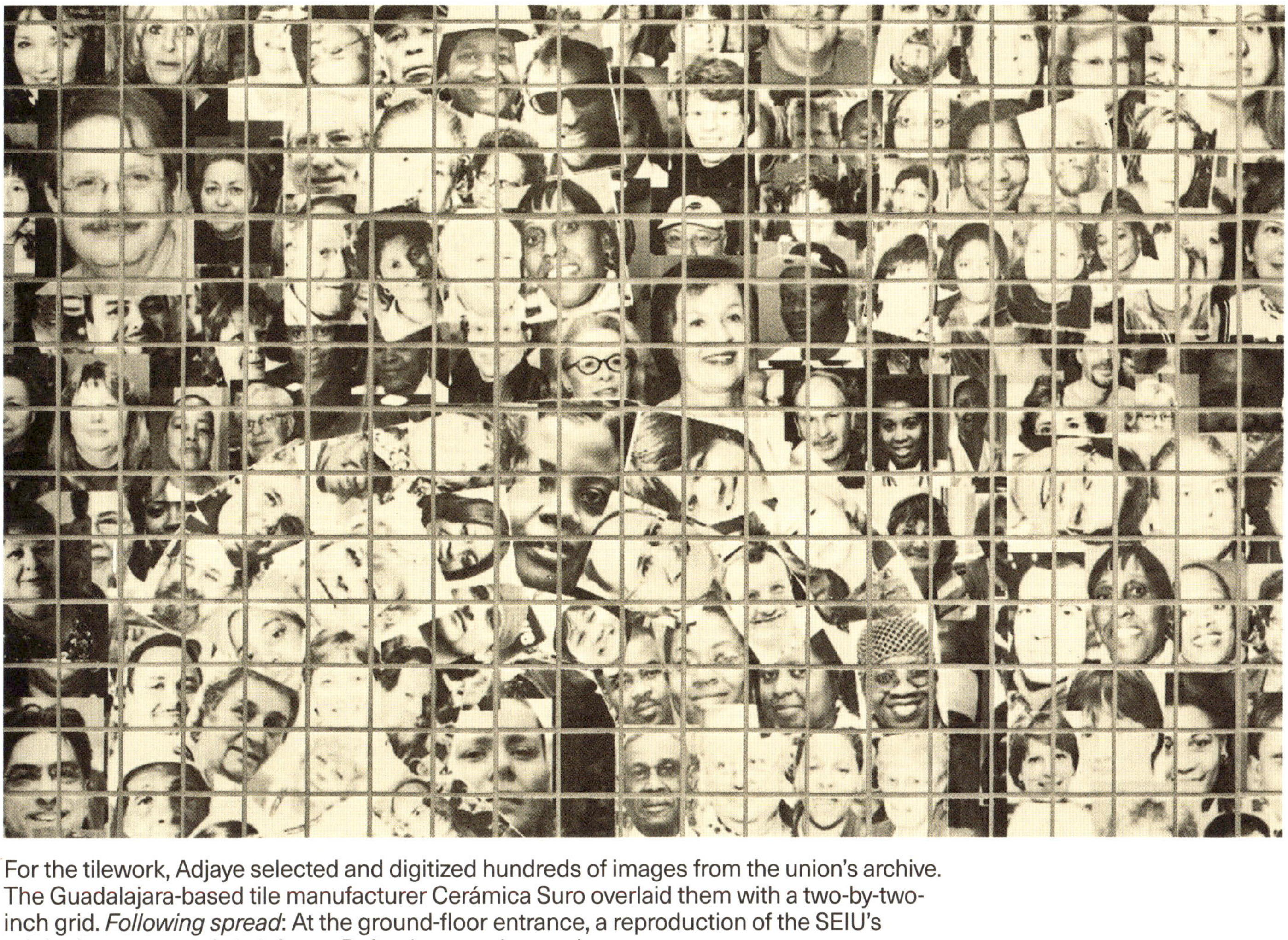

For the tilework, Adjaye selected and digitized hundreds of images from the union's archive. The Guadalajara-based tile manufacturer Cerámica Suro overlaid them with a two-by-two-inch grid. *Following spread*: At the ground-floor entrance, a reproduction of the SEIU's original monumental 1970 Anton Refregier mosaic mural.

If there is no struggle
there can be no progress
Frederick Douglass

130 William
New York, NY, US, 2021

130 William—Adjaye's first-ever skyscraper—cuts a provocative presence, boldly and elegantly inserting itself into the downtown Manhattan streetscape and skyline. Imagined as a vertical micro-city, the 66-story, 242-residence tower, in a roundabout way, embodies the architect's global perspective. Conceptually, in material, form, and feeling, it is reflective of a Lagos-meets-Rome-meets-New York purview, and of Adjaye's ability to rigorously investigate, expand upon, and tactfully reinterpret particular references. In stark contrast to the glass towers surrounding it, the building celebrates the masonry of the neighborhood's historic stonework high-rises (including 70 Pine Street, 20 Exchange Place, and the Woolworth Building), and with its soaring, rhythmically arranged arched windows, it recalls the city's early warehouses. Thinking of the tower form in terms of its relationship to nature, Adjaye was particularly inspired by termite mounds, the ecologies that exist within them, and the notion of using the earth to sculpt upward.

From afar, 130 William's distinctive silhouette draws the eyes in; up close, its many material details emerge. It is a sensorial structure of tactile delight. Built with a tinted hand-cast dark gray concrete facade—thick, textured panels intended to appear like volcanic rock—the monolithic building is, for Adjaye, a sort of material and philosophical continuation of his Sugar Hill mixed-use development (2015; page 46) in Harlem. And with its zigzag profile and tiered edges, slightly angled on each floor, the building's form also connects to that of the Smithsonian National Museum of African American History and Culture (2016; page 142) in Washington, DC.

An interplay between inside and outside exists throughout, starting on street level, which includes a public plaza. The lobby beckons with its mix of light and dark marble for the flooring and walls, including a cantilevered marble reception desk and slatted wood walls and an arched wood display case that allude to the building's facade. Inside the white oak–floored units, which range from studios to three-bedrooms (with penthouses featuring double-height loggias on the ten uppermost floors), there are custom burnished-bronze hardware and fittings that nod to the building's brass mullions and roof bulkhead, kitchens with Pietra Cardosa and Nero Marquina stone, and bathrooms with fluted Bianco Carrara or Grigio Versilia marble. Both engaging with the city and taking refuge from it, 130 William emphasizes the vast potential and potent power of tactility and texture in the twenty-first-century city.

A zigzag profile, not unlike the three-tiered corona of the Smithsonian National Museum of African American History and Culture (2016) in Washington, DC, runs up 130 Williams's sixty-six-floor exterior.

Beginning at the 56th floor, the loggias blur indoor and outdoor space, providing sweeping views across the city.

On the upper-terrace levels, the stone arches flip upside down, framing the cityscape beyond.

The texture of the dark gray, hand-casted concrete facade resembles volcanic rock.

Thick, arched windows recall the warehouse structures that once populated the Seaport neighborhood. *Following spread*: The black tower cuts a striking profile in downtown Manhattan, with sweeping views that include the East River and Brooklyn.

Winter Park Library
Winter Park, FL, US, 2021

Situated on a belvedere overlooking Lake Mendsen, in a 23-acre site that includes Martin Luther King Jr. Park, the Winter Park Library forms a monumental landmark and striking civic presence. Not only does the library and events center beckon visitors with its bold design, which takes aesthetic cues from regional fauna, it reckons with the Winter Park's complicated history (a racist infrastructure, with sides-of-the tracks segregation, was built into city's formation in the late 1800s). Replacing a previously existing library located to the city's east, it recalibrates its public realm toward the west. An advancement of Adjaye's philosophy of considering libraries as central community hubs and cultural catalyzers, the Winter Park project could be considered an extension of his two Idea Stores (2004 and 2005; page 208) in London and his two Washington, DC, public libraries (2012; pages 174 and 240, respectively).

Despite its 52,000-square-foot (4,830-square-meter) size and weighty structure, the project inserts—and asserts—itself on the site with poise and elegance. Designed to withstand hurricanes, while also bringing in natural light and providing sweeping views of the surrounding park through large windows, the campus exudes lightness and toughness at once. It features three vaulted structures made of a precast, rose-pigmented concrete framework, with large overhangs that provide necessary shade. Materially and tonally, the project loosely harks back to one of Adjaye's earliest, Concrete Garden (2001; page 29); it could also be considered a cousin to both Ruby City (2019; page 64) in San Antonio, Texas, and The Webster (2020; page 80) in Los Angeles.

A *porte-cochère*, or covered entry, welcomes visitors to the site, before opening up to the library, on the right, and the events center, on the left; beyond the buildings, a public-speaking stage jetties out, with steps coming down toward the water. In the two-story library, a flexible inner core with movable walls includes dedicated maker spaces, a "memory lab," private study areas, and an archive. Book stacks are arranged around the perimeter of both floors. The events center includes an auditorium, a ballroom, and a rooftop terrace. Both the library and events center flaunt dramatic, sculptural staircases. As if with arms outstretched, the project practically reaches out to the community to engage with it.

Three monumental rose-pigmented concrete pavilions rest on a raised belvedere. The cluster forms a new community anchor, inspired in part by local fauna and the region's vernacular architecture.

Inside the library, the subtle arches expressed on the exterior are revealed in the form of a dramatic interior ceiling.

As with Adjaye's Francis A. Gregory Neighborhood Library (2012) in Washington, DC, here large windows draw natural light deep into the interior. Flexible floor plates allow for a variety of spatial configurations.

A sculptural circular staircase, not unlike one at Adjaye's Smithsonian National Museum of African American History and Culture (2016) in Washington, DC, connects a ground-floor events center to a terrace and rehearsal rooms above.

Vaulted roof lines and extended windows of the first floor create a porous relationship between interior and exterior. *Following spread*: Located in Winter Park's Martin Luther King Jr. Park, the library and events center overlooks Lake Mendsen.

A *porte-cochère*, or covered entry, at the front of the site provides shelter and features an oculus that reveals glimpses of the sky.

A network of green spaces within Martin Luther King Jr. Park leads visitors to the library and events center.

Abrahamic Family House
Abu Dhabi, UAE, 2023

Inspired by the Document on Human Fraternity, the Abrahamic Family House brings together for the first time in world history a mosque, a church, and a synagogue on the same site, on Saadiyat Island, in the city's cultural district. Elevated on a plinth, the three spaces, each scaled at 130 feet (40 meters) high and with identical cubic proportions, are held up with architectural reverence for their distinctive traditions and histories, but also with no determinable hierarchy between them. Though there are differences in their screens and light-diffusion systems—as well as their cardinal directions (the church faces east, the mosque toward Mecca, the synagogue to Jerusalem)—the monumental site-cast concrete structures, hefty as they are, are connected through both a central Omani stone platform and a certain material lightness and fluidity. Considering the composition a "parametric fusion," Adjaye created philosophical links and inherent tensions within the form. A campus-scale mega site, in the vein of the Moscow School of Management SKOLKOVO (2010; page 230), the compound is designed as a literal and symbolic support system.

As with the Smithsonian National Museum of African American History and Culture (2016; page 142) in Washington, DC, the architecture here, too, becomes a metaphorical landmark of subconscious connections and narratives across time, but also, through the three structures, one of interfaith dialogue and coexistence. The plinth itself serves as a fourth building: a secular space called The Forum with outdoor courtyards, a library, and an exhibition space. Inspired by his memories of Middle Eastern architecture, the secluded courtyard of his Sunken House (2007) in London, and loosely referencing Jerusalem, Adjaye devised a podium structure that includes in its center "the Abrahamic hall," a cavernous space for contemplation made of rough acoustic earth plaster.

Rooted in Adjaye's early-career experimental pavilions, the site is a study of surface and form: At the church, vertical concrete bars on the exterior are echoed inside by a timber sculpture that hangs from the ceiling, recalling the excavated light of his Sclera Pavilion (2008; page 166). At the mosque, light passes through massive, swooping arches and hits an arabesque screen, the organically sculpted interior evoking monumental awe similar to that of Antoni Gaudí's Sagrada Familia church in Barcelona. At the synagogue, three layers of tree branch-like forms make up the facade's support, with an inner glass wall of stacked "V" beams beyond them. Inside, light streams in through a temple skylight and a thin metal screen that elegantly drapes from the roof. A triangular totem with engravings representing each religion stands tall at the center of the site—a welcoming, unifying marker.

The porous threshold between the secular space of the landscaped plinth and the Eminence Ahmed El-Tayeb Mosque provides an artfully articulated translation of the faith's iconography, which continues into the building's interior chamber.

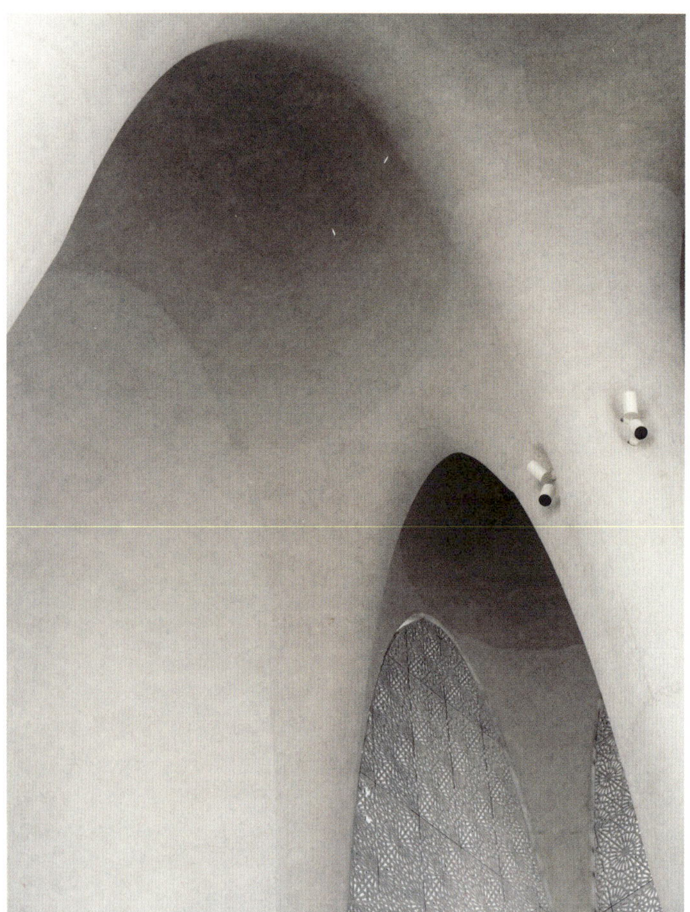

Top: Concrete forms in the mosque sculpt sunlight as it filters through mashrabiya screens, illuminating the *minbar*, or pulpit, with ephemeral patterns. *Bottom:* In the interior of the Moses Ben Maimon Synagogue, light glistens along a metal chainmail curtain, which recalls a Sukkot tent.

Expressed through equal space ratios, the complex's three houses of faith are unified in material and proportion. The exterior of the synagogue is defined by a pattern of diagonal concrete branches and "V" beams, creating a frame for an inner glass wall that allows light to illuminate the inside.

Top: Framed by the landscaped grounds of the plinth, the facade of His Holiness Francis Church is articulated by a series of vertical bars that dissolve once inside the light-filled space. *Bottom:* Reminiscent of the altar at St. Peter's Basilica in the Vatican, the church's interior is defined by a timber sculpture dramatically suspended from the ceiling.

Metal

Bernie Grant Arts Center

London, UK, 2007

Piety Bridge and Wharf

New Orleans, LA, US, 2014

Aïshti Foundation

Beirut, LB, 2015

Smithsonian National Museum of African American History and Culture

Washington, DC, US, 2016

Metal holds a special, quite untypical place within David Adjaye's practice. In the architect's hands, rather than simply serving as something weighty, aluminum and steel can take on a sort of weightlessness or, through ornamentation, an ethereality. Sometimes integrated in the form of a screen—as in both the Aïshti Foundation (2015) in Beirut, Lebanon, and the Smithsonian National Museum of African American History and Culture (2016) in Washington, DC—metal becomes a frame, or a "climate moderator," between inside and outside. Emotional top layers, the perforated metal facades of both Aïshti and the NMAAHC, each wrapped around glass, are multifaceted environmental filters for light to pour through. They could also be considered architectural sieves for observation and contemplation. In the case of the NMAAHC, the screen converses directly with the National Mall, the Washington Monument, and the surrounding area's neoclassical blocks; the Aïshti screen functions similarly at its site along the Mediterranean Sea. With both, Adjaye is actively searching for and investigating a new kind of ornamental construction, one deep in metaphor and meaning. Extending out of African and Middle Eastern traditions, and unabashedly confident and original in their statement-making, these screens are his way of tackling head-on the assumption in contemporary architecture of ornament as frivolous. Both engage deeply in narrative, but subtly and without being too on the nose: the NMAAHC's form references ancient Yoruban sculpture and its elegantly shaped aluminum panels the ironwork of enslaved people in the American South, while the Aïshti's bright red zigzagging exterior irreverently evokes the Red Sea.

Because of its weathering power, Adjaye is also particularly fascinated with Cor-Ten steel as a primary material. The universality of iron ore—the fact that it comes from and exists in the cosmos, or, in Adjaye's words, "*is* the constitution of the universe"—appeals greatly to the architect for both its elemental attributes and metaphorical qualities. For Adjaye, the meaning of a material is just as important as the physical thing itself. More than stainless steel or other alloys, Cor-Ten steel, with its tendency to naturally oxidize and bleed color, connects deeply to the notion of alchemy, shifting in hues and tones over time—a living, ever-changing thing in the world. With both LN House (2008) in Denver, Colorado, and the Piety Bridge and Wharf (2014) in New Orleans, Adjaye intentionally allows for the morphability of Cor-Ten to shine. At LN House, the decoloration of the metal acts as a striking meteorological measurer. Disrupting and accenting the bland everydayness of the neighboring streetscape in a welcoming way—and in refreshing contrast to his glass-paneled Museum of Contemporary Art Denver (2007) next door—the home's exterior magnetically pulls in onlookers with its rough-hewn texture. As with Adjaye's stone and concrete constructions, there is a relic quality to his Cor-Ten projects.

With the Bernie Grant Arts Center (2007) in London—which Adjaye views as an informal, non-ornamental twin of Aïshti—metal has become a tool with which the architect explores the subtle compression within a given building or structure. For Piety Bridge, Adjaye created an elegant arched form at once grounded and heavy-looking. Contextually spot-on, it appears as if it has been on the site for decades, extending out of the neighboring landscape along the Mississippi River, but also, because of its tension and suspension, practically floating and weightless. Through various applications, Adjaye shows that, even despite its apparent rigidity, metal can have incredible breadth and fluidity.

Bernie Grant Arts Center
London, UK, 2007

Built in memory of Bernie Grant (1944–2000), born in Guyana and the UK's first Black member of Parliament, the Bernie Grant Arts Center is at once a memorial, a community hub, a performance arts venue, and a neighborhood incubator. Established by Haringey Council and a trust in Grant's name, the 43,300-square-foot (4,025-square-meter) complex, located in North London's Tottenham Green ward, was created, in part, to develop strategies for tackling institutional racism. For Adjaye, the project offered an opportunity to embody not only Grant's Guyanese roots and strong local presence through form and material (purpleheart and heat-treated timber, in particular), but also to showcase an African spirit of invention and celebrate the local area's multiethnic vibrancy. Inspired by the interconnected way that shacks are built in many shantytowns, while also engaging head-on with the site's protected Edwardian architecture, Adjaye sought to form a shared landscape through an assembly of parts.

Working with and around a listed, three-story historic structure at the site's entrance that once housed public baths, Adjaye melded to its backside a modern black ceramic-clad box—his way of helping introduce and integrate the building's brickwork and stone with two adjacent contemporary pavilions. The site's centerpiece, just beyond, is an elegantly arched, shedlike auditorium that includes a 274-seat performance space and a rehearsal studio. Its east-facing roof cantilevers dramatically, revealing a double-height foyer; in concert with its optically patterned extruded metal facade, ribs of wood cladding extend from inside the foyer out, drawing the eye in and beckoning passersby to enter. The third building, a long, narrow edifice called the Enterprise Center, wedged into the rear of the campus, comprises a dance studio and twenty spaces for local businesses.

Materially, each building features a steel-frame construction with a concrete base and employs cladding reflective of its purpose and position on the site. Playing with various material effects of metal, stone, and wood throughout, the three-building ensemble uses continuous patterns to distort perceptions and sensitively merge the campus with the surrounding area. Both literally and figuratively reflective, the Bernie Grant Arts Center and its material palette are an architectural meditation on the very notion of reflection.

The welcoming "hood" of the center's main theater building is clad in purpleheart timber, common in Guyana, where the project's namesake, Bernie Grant, was born. The administration building, partially seen in the right foreground, features a black ceramic rainscreen, which contrasts with the red brick of the original structure.

The north and south facades of the main theater building are wrapped in alternating bands of ribbed, powder-coated steel. A resulting moiré effect gives an unexpected lightness to the structure.

The steel panels on the facade of the main theater building are arranged in three different heights, creating a sense of weightlessness and practically dissolving its vertical scale.

Above and *following spread*: Wood cladding extends from the interior spaces to the outside, bridging indoors and out and drawing visitors and passersby into the warm, hearth-like environment inside.

Piety Bridge and Wharf
New Orleans, LA, US, 2014

Built in the Bywater neighborhood of New Orleans in the aftermath of Hurricane Katrina and as part of a larger master plan for revitalizing the city and its riverfront, Piety Bridge and Wharf serve as key focal points of—and the former, a symbolic entryway to—Crecent Park. Providing public access to the formerly industrial stretch of riverfront, the 1.4-mile (2.25-kilometer) park includes a 20-acre landscaped network of bike paths, playgrounds, and a dog run, as well as two adaptively reused wharfs.

Made of Cor-Ten steel, Piety Bridge fans out over active train tracks and a flood wall, with timber steps leading up and then down toward the Mississippi River (or, upon exit, toward Chartres Street); its elegantly arranged steel walls, which subtly scale up in height, peak in the middle, creating a chasm of compression and expansion. Eliminating views of the city, the sculptural footbridge slows down those who walk across it, its form calling for a breath, a pause, a moment of contemplation. It is not only a functional metal arch, but is also in many ways a monument—a meditative, low-key landmark that pays homage to the city's industrial and maritime pasts while creating something entirely new and uplifting. The site's visual anchor, the bridge evokes a sense of transcendence.

At the reimagined Piety Wharf, which occupies the footprint of a former warehouse, Adjaye merges old and new. Maintaining a concrete remnant of the building that once stood at the site, intentionally kept as a raw reminder, he established a ghostly, minimalist memorial to what was, and a backdrop for the wharf's expansive wood-planked plaza, featuring a series of reddish concrete benches and plinths, accented and framed by weathered steel posts and guardrails. The skeletal wooden frame remains of another wharf along the waterline add to the site's post-industrial edge. Similar to the McCarter Switching Station (2018; page 56) in Newark, New Jersey, Piety Bridge and Wharf turn what would otherwise have been ignored or considered a blight into a central space for public engagement and civic pride.

The Piety Bridge arch rises over a freight railroad line and down to the New Orleans waterfront. The material choice of Cor-Ten steel honors and celebrates the site's industrial and maritime past.

Top: Piety Street and the Bywater neighborhood of New Orleans, as seen from the top of the bridge. *Bottom*: The bridge grants access to Crescent Park, which includes this industrial wharf, adapted for public use, along the Mississippi River.

In visual dialogue with Piety Bridge, the wharf becomes a viewing platform and, as with the bridge, features weathering Cor-Ten steel. *Following spread*: An active train track runs underneath the bridge, along with Crescent Park's trails and native plantings.

TX 728841
PY 29130 US GAL
PY 110250L

Aïshti Foundation
Beirut, LB, 2015

Stretched out between a seaside promenade and a densely packed twelve-lane roadway, the Aïshti Foundation cuts a striking figure on the Beirut cityscape. Comprising retail shops, a bookstore, restaurants, cafés, a spa, and a rooftop bar, the mixed-use complex also houses a private contemporary art museum for the collection of its owner, Tony Salamé, the founder of the Lebanese luxury retailer Aïshti. Prior to beginning work on the project, Adjaye spent several days in Italy with Salamé, during which they traveled to buildings designed by Gio Ponti, and indeed there is a hint of Ponti in the building's gridded graphic design and ceramic red facade.

Extending out of a material language that Adjaye began to develop with the Bernie Grant Arts Center (2007; page 121) in London—the idea of a system of metal extrusions—Aïshti serves, in the architect's mind, as a bookend to that early project. Developed at the same time as the Smithsonian National Museum of African American History and Culture (2016; page 142) in Washington, DC, Aïshti similarly features an ornamental aluminum screen clad around a glass box, and, as with the NMAAHC's relationship to the National Mall and its artifacts inside, its outside layer reflects its specific coastal city locale.

A project by the sea and of the sea, Aïshti was built to be both contextual and symbolic. Cheekily, its red exoskeleton is a subtle but bold play on the very idea of the Red Sea; it also alludes to the shade of red on many of Lebanon's traditional brick roofs, and isn't too far off from the color found in the horizontal stripes of the country's flag. Featuring a digitally designed ziggurat pattern that Adjaye drew from an abstracted ocean image, the screen is cut into a series of tube sections that create a sense of rippling motion; on the eastern side of the exterior, a large window opens up views to the waterfront and surrounding cityscape. Inside, arranged around a central atrium with an Escher-esque array of escalators and walkways, are the retail floors, where, through the use of a skylight and multiple mirrored surfaces, a reflective, watery quality pervades. A sweeping architectural gesture, Aïshti merges art and retail to create a setting emblematic of the rich and dynamic layers of its home city.

A louvered red aluminum frame wraps around the Aïshti Foundation building's exterior, reflecting its relationship to the surrounding Mediterranean Sea.

Top: The geometric "thunderbolt" pattern, drawn from an abstracted ocean image, gives the bold building a transitory and ephemeral feel. *Bottom*: The dynamic facade, as seen from across a busy adjacent roadway.

Top: An interior view framing the Mediterranean Sea. *Bottom*: The ceiling of the retail section creates an ethereal shopping environment between sky, sea, and city.

The building's highly reflective central atrium projects natural light deep into its M.C. Escher-esque shopping arcade.

A void between the building and its screen, seen here from an industrial plant next door, gives the building a weightless appearance within its dense portside locale. *Following spread*: The foundation's seemingly disparate programs of art and retail are integrated through a cohesive tiled design that presents a continuous language throughout the exterior.

Smithsonian National Museum of African American History and Culture Washington DC, US, 2016

Just 800 feet (245 meters) northeast of the Washington Monument, the Smithsonian National Museum of African American History and Culture (NMAAHC) rises up, resilient, as if emerging from the ground. In contrast with Washington, DC's surrounding neoclassical white-marble norm, the metal-sheathed NMAAHC expresses a new, multi-layered architectural narrative. Clad in 3,600 bronze-colored cast-aluminum panels, it is an emotion-filled building of meaning, feeling, and healing. An abstract, contextually astute symbol, the NMAAHC carries a strong but quiet presence despite its 350,000-square-foot (33,000-square-meter) size. At once reflective and responsive, contemplative and provocative, it does not impose or call out for attention; instead, it is a discrete structure that emphasizes its distinctive silhouette. With a dark black-brown facade that absorbs light and shimmers in the sun, it stands defiant, proud, and hopeful.

On the exterior, metaphor and meaning abound: the three-tiered "corona" lattice that wraps the building was inspired by Yoruban art from West Africa; its materiality and pattern reference ironwork once done by enslaved people in the American South; and the cantilevered "porch" and water feature on the building's south side, connecting inside and out, link back to architectural roots in Africa, the Caribbean, and the American South. Directly in conversation with the Washington Monument, each panel on the facade is tilted outward at 17.5 degrees, matching the angle of the Monument's crown.

Inside, visitors are guided from the bottom to the top, upward through a subterranean complex of galleries; past a 300-seat theater and café; through a vast, light-filled reception area, atrium, and shop; and finally, to two upper-floor galleries. Throughout, a diverse material palette—precast concrete, timber, black-brown terrazzo floors and stairs, and a glazed skin—elevates the atmosphere, with dappled natural light dramatically filtering in during the day.

That more than half of the ten-level building—as much a memorial as a museum—is hidden below ground is fitting: this institution houses artifacts deeply embedded in the history of America that testify to stories and pasts long brushed over, and at last presented on the national stage. (The NMAAHC took nearly a century to form and complete, overcoming countless bureaucratic roadblocks.) Literally and figuratively uplifting, the building serves as an architectural antidote that recenters Black and African American people and helps fill a massive historical void and cultural chasm.

Echoing the museum's mission and its site on the National Mall, the building's intricate metal lattice, inspired in part by Yoruban art, is angled 17.5 degrees outward, to align with the neighboring Washington Monument's pyramidal crown.

Top: A monumental circular metal staircase is located at the pivotal point in the building, where visitors can descend into the History Galleries below ground or ascend to the Community and Culture Galleries above. *Bottom*: A massive, cantilevered porch and reflecting pool look out onto the National Monument, offering a moment for reflection and respite.

Top: Extending the height of the building, the detailed metal screen composes an array of shadow patterns in the atrium inside. *Bottom*: Sunlight falls through a ground-level oculus and into a contemplative, chapel-like memorial space featuring a ring of falling water.

Situated on the National Mall, the museum's porous metal and glass facade contrasts the neighboring neoclassical, typically solid white marble structures.

The vast, column-free space provides a weightless and ethereal feel as visitors are guided through an emotional historical journey.

Terraced floors highlight the ornamental bronze-coated aluminum screen, which was modulated to control sunlight and transparency, and designed in a pattern that references historical African American craftsmanship.

The metal panels, supported by architecturally exposed steel frames, seemingly float in place. *Following spread*: The design of the building is rooted in metaphor, reflecting upon its place both in American history and on the Washington Mall.

Coated with a bronze pigment that was applied by hand to form textural variations, the panels allow for fluid material expressions and sensory effects that change depending on time of day, weather, and sun exposure.

Wood

Horizon Pavilion
London, UK, 2007

Sclera Pavilion
London, UK, 2008

William O. Lockridge/ Bellevue Library
Washington, DC, US, 2012

Gwangju River Reading Room
Gwangju, KR, 2013

IBA Hamburg
Hamburg, DE, 2013

Ever since his time as a master's student at the Royal College of Art, in the early 1990s, David Adjaye has used wood as a primary element in his work. He has always appreciated timber for its long-lasting, gracefully aging, and carbon-neutral qualities, as well as for the tactile ways in which it plays with light, and he has encouraged clients to use it for these reasons. In his firm's earlier years, timber played an especially important role in the material development of his practice when, unable to find many clients who would use the material, he began making both temporary and permanent pavilions with it. Each structure served as a sort of first-principles study. The resulting "art-ish" (Adjaye's word) environments—explorations of the illumination of space, the creation of atmosphere, and the contrast between dark and light—provided visitors with a sense of visceral delight.

Among the earliest of these structures was the Your Black Horizon Art Pavilion, created in collaboration with the Icelandic Danish artist Olafur Eliasson, which was installed in Venice in 2005, and then in Lopud, Croatia, in 2007; it comprised a long, naturally lit hallway that led into a dark rectangular gallery space in which a mid-height light installation by Eliasson, representing a horizon line, created an ever-changing optical illusion. At night, the structure would itself become, as is the case with so much of Adjaye's work, a beacon-like lightbox.

His next major pavilion, Horizon (2007–2008), an hourglass-shaped space installed in London and Rome, extended this concept through a study of wood joinery and the extended view. With the Sclera Pavilion (2008) in London, Adjaye created a wood study of excavation, or subtraction; carving away two circles, he quite literally split the incoming light, practically physicalizing the light itself and creating what he calls "frozen motion." Other wood pavilions from this period include the Specere Pavilion (2009) at Scotland's Kielder National Park, the Genesis Pavilion (2011) in Miami, and the Ephemeropteræ Pavilion (2012) in Vienna. Each served as "my kind of private Idaho," Adjaye says, freeing the architect to be unconstrained and dream of new possibilities with wood.

Furthering this work, Adjaye's Gwangju Reading Room (2013), a memorial in South Korea, merges a pagoda-like timber canopy with a concrete plinth, which in turn is subtly integrated into a hydrodynamic site along the banks of the Gwangju River. At the William O. Lockridge/Bellevue Library (2012) in Washington, DC, timber mullions fulfill a unifying function, tying together the inside and the outside, and becoming the visual focal point. Though the building is also made of concrete and glass, it stands out as a decidedly wood construction.

Perhaps the most resolutely timber project in Adjaye's portfolio is the IBA Hamburg (2013) in Germany, a prefabricated, eleven-unit social-housing development. An expanded version of earlier wood-clad residential projects—Elektra House (1999), Lost House (2004), and Sunken House (2007)—IBA is a generous cube form that creates "new extractions," as Adjaye puts it. Honoring the power and potential of wood by putting it at the forefront, the building highlights the versatility, flexibility, and ecological advantages inherent in working with the material. With the IBA, Adjaye shows that harnessing wood in a particular way can lead toward a more egalitarian architecture.

Horizon Pavilion
London, UK, 2007

In the mid-2000s, when the London gallerist Michael Hue-Williams approached Adjaye about presenting an exhibition of his work, the architect responded by suggesting he make an energy-neutral timber pavilion for the show as a "pure thought." Thinking back to his time as a Royal College of Art student in the early 1990s, during which he studied in Japan and proposed an all-timber building for his thesis, Adjaye was inspired to create a simple screen-like construction out of spruce, combining two intersecting triangles on a central axis via a lapped, horizontal–vertical joint. Through repetition of this joint, the architect created the Horizon Pavilion's walls, structure, and texture, all unified with a black stain. In many respects, the project could be viewed as a contemporary case study on Jun'ichirō Tanizaki's 1933 book *In Praise of Shadows*, a paean to the power of contrasting light and dark.

Built around an entrance sequence that forms a meditative space and leads toward a vista, the original Horizon installation—in a basement gallery and artificially backlit (its only source of illumination)—included an infinity-view photograph of the Sea of Galilee, taken by Adjaye, that served as a serene reveal, practically turning the structure into a waterside teahouse. A physical embodiment of key elements in Adjaye's design practice—light and shadow, heft, materiality and tactility, the creation of atmosphere—Horizon was an architectural acknowledgment of the essential relationship between a structure and its surroundings, as well as a celebration of the importance of framing a view.

A precedent to landscape-oriented projects that put vistas front and center, such as the Specere Pavilion in Scotland's Kielder National Park (2009) and the Nkron villa (2012) in Gomoa Fetteh, Ghana, Horizon also served as a capstone of sorts to the traveling exhibition *David Adjaye: Form, Heft, Material*, curated by Okwui Enwezor and Zoë Ryan and shown at the Haus der Kunst in Munich, the Art Institute of Chicago, and the Garage Museum of Art in Moscow. Another variation on its design is the triangular-prism Genesis Pavilion, first presented at the entrance to the Design Miami fair in 2011; now covered in a creosote preservative, it is installed at the home of the Miami developer Craig Robins. Horizon itself is now located at Hue-Williams's Albion Fields sculpture park in Oxfordshire, England.

Previous spread: The pavilion, as installed at the Albion Fields sculpture park in Oxfordshire. *Top*: The edge of the pavilion, with its view looking out at the verdant park. *Bottom*: The slots in the timber pavilion filter and diffuse the light, creating an interior of overlapping shadows.

Top: A black wood stain unifies the spruce structure, originally installed in the Albion Gallery in London in 2007. *Bottom:* In its permanent home, the pavilion interacts with the surrounding environment through its ever-changing shadows, according to the natural light.

The repetition and depth of the timber screen creates a gradation of light, shown here at the Albion Gallery in 2007.

A backlit vista provides the only source of illumination, also highlighting the pavilion's transparency. *Following spread:* The pavilion, as installed for the *David Adjaye: Form, Heft, Material* exhibition at Haus der Kunst in Munich, Germany, in 2015.

28

Sclera Pavilion
London, UK, 2008

Built as part of the 2008 London Design Festival, the Sclera Pavilion was situated in a square within the Southbank Center arts complex, near the London Eye observation wheel along the River Thames. Inspired by the human eye, Adjaye created a 39-by-26-foot (12-by-8-meter) structure intended to play with visual perception through material, form, and space. Made of American tulipwood—then newly available for external use as a result of modern impregnation techniques—the oval-shape design (later sold in a Phillips de Pury auction) was an intimate study in the structural potential and visual properties of the material.

For Adjaye, the project was largely a way of making space by extraction. Rather than the addition of material, it was about cutting away and shaping light—or, effectively, the notion of architecture as sculpture. A two-plane construction, the pavilion was created by carving away two circles, or "crop-outs," and then excavating further from there. A profound, mind-expanding lesson for the architect, the phenomenological result would inform much of his work to come. When it comes to architectural engagement with light, no project has had a greater impact on Adjaye. Stalactite-like forms dramatically came down from the ceiling, allowing little gaps of daylight to filter through in an exquisite distribution of matter and light, becoming an almost singular material experience.

Sclera's cutaway approach is something that Adjaye has sought to integrate, on various levels, into nearly every building since, notably the original (though never built) hanging wood ceiling installation for the atrium of the Smithsonian National Museum of African American History and Culture (2016; page 142) in Washington, DC and the church for the Abrahamic Family House interfaith complex (2023; page 116) in Abu Dhabi. Suggesting the visual qualities of the eye itself through its circular form, Sclera celebrated the ability of wood—when elegantly molded to integrate daylight—to encourage reflection and meaning through seeing.

Top: Almost fort-like from the outside, the Sclera Pavilion features an oval mass that dissolves through the subtraction of the material. *Bottom:* Inside, rhythmic openings provide glimpses of the London streetscape beyond. *Following spread*: The suspended ceiling's cascade of tulipwood reconsitutes the viewer's notion of form and space as they cross the pavilion's threshold to the outside world.

Inspired by the human eye (and aptly temporarily installed near the London Eye), the pavilion's material composition contorts light and shadow and inventively plays with visual perception. *Following spread*: The elevated foundation of the pavilion grants views of the bustling city just beyond its undulating walls, while creating a quiet interior retreat for visitors.

William O. Lockridge/Bellevue Library Washington, DC, US, 2012

Shortly after Adjaye won the commission to design the Smithsonian Museum of African American History and Culture (2016; page 142) on the National Mall, he was approached by Washington, DC's public library system to design two libraries in the city's southwest Ward 8 district. Nestled in a sloping site, the multitiered William O. Lockridge/Bellevue Library—finished months after the nearby Francis A. Gregory Library (2012; page 240)—forms a striking civic presence within the surrounding residential neighborhood of modest wood and brick houses. As much an information center as a community hub, the Lockridge project (as with the Gregory one) extends from, and is conceptually similar to, Adjaye's two early-career Idea Stores (2004 and 2005; page 208) in London. Not unlike the brutalist concrete-and-glass designs of the British architects Alison and Peter Smithson, under whom Adjaye once studied at London's Royal College of Art, the podlike structure, through its rigorous combination of material and form, functions as a "climate moderator."

Arranged into a geometric cluster of identical rectangles across three floors—a stout central concrete core, plus three elevated, pedestal-mounted volumes jutting out above—the sculptural structure handily accommodates the site's hilly topography, which drops in grade about 40 feet (12 meters), and also establishes a covered area for outdoor gatherings. On its east side, the library features glazed ground-to-ceiling walls that bring in natural light, the primary source of illumination. Inside the main pavilion, a rectilinear light well pierces through the green-tinted middle, inviting light down into it, while a concrete staircase stretches between the second and third floors. Throughout the interior, judicious juxtapositions of material and color—red-floored corridors, black-glass staff rooms, yellow-walled circulation areas—playfully orient visitors.

While decidedly rooted in concrete, the project puts a heightened emphasis on wood—a unifying material that pulls the structure together, framing views, adding texture, and establishing an intimate sense of scale that belies the building's 22,500-square-foot (2,090-square-meter) footprint. With the insertion of a centralized system of vertical, rhythmically arranged cedar fins, the design softens boundaries and shifts visitors' perceptions: inside and outside merge and converge. The neighborhood beyond becomes a material part of the project, and vice versa.

Wrapped in concrete and glass, the library's structure stands out most for its timber fins that not only fulfill structural and shading requirements but articulate the vertical presence of the building.

Opposite: Like the branches of a firmly rooted tree, the geometries of the clustered volumes jut out over the sloping site, forming a series of shifting rectangles that maximize filtered natural light. *Above:* The exposed concrete interior balances the warm wood exterior.

The exterior cedar fins are visible amongst the colorful and reflective interiors.

The layered nature of the building's interior is heightened by the use of reflective glass partitions to form separate spaces.

Natural light floods the interior, creating a sense of expansion within the intimately scaled building.

Echoing the interior, the boundary between building and environment practically dissolves through the use of glass that mirrors the tree-lined neighborhood. *Following spread*: Small, medium, and large forms mediate the scale of the building and accomodate the surrounding landscape.

115

Gwangju River Reading Room
Gwangju, KR, 2013

A memorial to the two hundred students of Chonnam National University who, in May 1980, demonstrated against the state of martial law imposed by the government, and in turn were fired upon and killed, the Gwangju River Reading Room was designed to be a somber, weighty setting in which to reflect, mourn, and remember. Composed of two materials, timber and concrete, and embedded along a hydrodynamic site on the banks of the Gwangju River, the black-colored structure is at once emotionally charged and ecologically integrated. Built to accommodate high tide, its concrete base allows for the pavilion to become semi-submerged, with its ribbed wood top effectively becoming a table atop the river.

The pavilion is architecture as percolator. A wide, geometric staircase dramatically leads visitors from a street-level promenade above down to the waterfront, providing access to the grassy floodplain below, which becomes a seasonal park. Its cavelike base structure appears almost as if carved from the earth. A modern-day interpretation of Korean pagoda pastiche, and inspired by the various timber building traditions Adjaye saw during his time in Japan, the arched, four-sided cover extends from the architect's early pavilion "tests," such as Horizon (2007; page 157) and Sclera (2008; page 166), especially in its exploration of material, form, light, and shadow.

Commissioned by artistic director Nikolaus Hirsch and curators Philipp Misselwitz and Eui Young Chun as part of the 2013 Gwangju Biennale (and one of eight follies created by artists and architects for the occasion), Adjaye collaborated on the project with the British-American writer and photographer Taiye Selasi. Built to house a library of two hundred human-rights books selected by Selasi, the pavilion features four ground-level pillars with cut-out square and rectangular bookshelves, each to be intentionally filled with a different book—clear, visible representations of each protestor who lost their life, all connected through a singular form. (More shelves are arranged along the central staircase and the outer walls at its base.) On the upper level, tables and seating invite a variety of uses. Like the student demonstrators it memorializes, the pavilion boldly takes over public space in an act of mobilization and exchange.

Composed of a wood canopy that rests atop a concrete base, the pavilion features an intentional material juncture that delineates the high-tide mark of the Gwangju River. At high tide, the structure becomes a "table" that seemingly floats above the water.

The four-sided timber structure is a nod to traditional Korean pagodas. Arches on each side rise off the concrete base to join in the center, forming a central reading area, with the bases themselves functioning as bookshelves.

Simple wood joinery techniques give the canopy its elegant form and rhythmic texture. *Following spread:* A walkway underneath the pavilion's stairs forms a portal-like passageway and shelter.

IBA Hamburg
Hamburg, DE, 2013

Commissioned in 2007 as part of an international design exhibition and urban development project comprising "sensitive interventions" and low-cost, energy-efficient prototypes in Hamburg, Germany, in and around the Elbe Islands, IBA Hamburg pushes forward Adjaye's early-career London explorations of timber architecture—starting with Elektra House (1999) and followed by Lost House (2004) and Sunken House (2007) —into a relatively compact, 12,400-square-foot (1,150-square-meter) residential construction. Located in the city's Wilhelmsburg district, the four-story structure is made up of a sculpted solid timber cube, much of it prefabricated and built in just four weeks. Featuring a building-block design with same-sized, quickly assemblable modules stacked around a central circulation core, it allows for flexible layouts: nine apartments ranging from two to four rooms and 500 to 1,350 square feet (47 to 124 square meters) in size, as well as two "maisonettes." Every unit includes a loggia. Similar to Sunken House, as well as the steel-covered LN House (2008) in Denver, Colorado, the case-study design plays with the notion of a monolithic structure punctuated with extractions—its recessed terraces, slatted surfaces, and window openings establish a rhythmic interplay of light and shadow across its vertical and horizontal forms.

Seeking to demonstrate how wood can be used at scale across a multi-occupant apartment complex, Adjaye created a dynamic, ecologically minded design that exudes a strong material presence. IBA Hamburg is a resolutely timber construction, clad in dried, fire-treated larch panels. Inside, it features a composite structure of wood and concrete that spans the supporting walls, allowing for flexible layouts. Other than its solid concrete floor slab, wood is used throughout. The windows are arranged around the sun, with the number varying depending on the direction they face. An architecture of reduction, the project shows off its material aura and suggests that timber can be as substantial and practical as brick, glass, metal, or concrete.

The horizontal larch wood struts break up the monolithic form of the building.

The prefabricated wood and slabs of reinforced concrete allow for a variety of unit types, each with their own suspended private terrace.

Wood is used extensively throughout the building's interior, including on the floors and ceilings of the units. *Following spread*: The box-shaped building and its piano key-like window slats form a striking presence, with its "stacked" construction allowing for various apartment sizes and configurations.

Located on Germany's largest river island, the luminous timber building subtly references the site's natural ecology.

Glass

Within Reach at Venice Biennale
Venice, IT, 2003

Idea Store Chrisp Street
London, UK, 2004

Idea Store Whitechapel Road
London, UK, 2005

Stephen Lawrence Center
London, UK, 2007

Museum of Contemporary Art Denver
Denver, CO, US, 2007

Moscow School of Management SKOLKOVO
Moscow, RU, 2010

Francis A. Gregory Neighborhood Library
Washington, DC, US, 2012

Unlike so many of the soulless modern-day glass structures common in cities around the world today, Adjaye's glass buildings bring a textural, reflective quality to the material that indicates sensitivity and a human touch. Adjaye's approach to glass, in many ways, reflects on the very notion of reflection. While he admires the Modernist buildings of Mies van der Rohe—particularly his clean-lined, glass-walled courtyard houses—Adjaye refutes the Miesian conceit that glass equals an absence of material, simply serving as a membrane. Instead, he embraces the weighty qualities of glass, particularly its crystalline nature and its ability to harness, diffuse, manipulate, refract, and reflect light inside a building and across its surfaces. Adjaye's glass structures should not be called "light and airy;" through his particular use of the material, he intentionally brings a sense of heft to it.

With glass, Adjaye quite literally draws in light, physicalizing it, often playing with color and offering it back to the visitor in an awe-inspiring, constantly shifting spectrum. Built in direct conversation with the sun and oriented around it, his glass buildings connect not only to the outside world, but to the cosmos and the far beyond. Allowing for light to shift throughout the day, Adjaye's glass buildings plan for—and play with—cold and warm light; morning, afternoon, and dusk light; various seasonal coloration shifts; and a wide range of atmospheric conditions. While this is certainly the case at the metal-curtained, glass-walled Smithsonian National Museum of African American History and Culture (2016) in Washington, DC, perhaps no Adjaye project captures the spirit of this to profound effect more than his sprawling Moscow School of Management, SKOLKOVO (2010), in Russia. Designed as a contemporary citadel, the floating-disk mega-structure effectively functions as a compass. Featuring seven pixelated patterns, the building's facade creates an array of spectral effects throughout the day.

The Idea Stores on Chrisp Street and Whitechapel Road (2004 and 2005, respectively) in London similarly play with patterned glass as a semiporous reflective layer between inside and out, at once inviting and protective. At the Stephen Lawrence Center (2007) in London, Adjaye composed a design based on a drawing by the artist Chris Ofili, combining glass and metal mesh to form a red memorial "lantern." Built in honor of Stephen Lawrence, an architecture student murdered in London in 1993, its red glow at night and ornamental shadows establish a feeling at once ethereal and eerie—one that would later inform, to different effect, the light and shadow play at the NMAAHC.

The notion of a building as a lightbox is also alive at the Museum of Contemporary Art Denver (2007), which, when lit up at night appears, in the context of the streetscape, the architectural equivalent of a soft-glowing paper lamp. At the Francis A. Gregory Neighborhood Library (2012) in Washington, DC, which Adjaye calls "the ultimate wood temple," he used glass to pay homage to the landscape outside, and to once again create spectral effects. In concert with timber and a steel-frame construction, the abstract geometric glass facade, made by using parametric tools, gets away from any idea of "transparency," and instead celebrates glass for its extraordinary ability to imbue a building with feeling.

Within Reach at the Venice Biennale Venice, IT, 2003

In the early 1990s, Adjaye and the British artist Chris Ofili were classmates at the Royal College of Art, and as Adjaye was beginning his practice, Ofili asked him to design a home and studio for him in London's East End. The project was completed in 1999, the year after Ofili won the Turner Prize. The two became longtime friends and collaborators, next working together on *The Upper Room* (2002), an exquisitely arranged installation at Tate Britain and a clear embodiment of the reverence and respect between the architect and the artist.

In 2003, the two partnered on another powerful project, *Within Reach*, for the British Pavilion at that year's Venice Biennale. Since 2000, Ofili had been working on a series of red, black, and green paintings—glittering, resin-layered works based on the colors of the pan-African union flag—featuring two "Afromantics," a hero and a heroine. Adjaye saturated the pavilion's timber walls and floor carpets in these same colors, forming a "sacred jungle," as he puts it. Upon arriving, visitors entered through a black tunnel that established a neutral space. In the main gallery, Ofili sought to engulf the exhibition's centermost painting in light and establish a sort of radiating "celestial body" around it. Adjaye's response was to design a glass sculpture, called *Afro Kaleidoscope*, that covered the pavilion's central skylight. Using early computer-modeling software, and with engineering help from the Sri Lankan-British designer Cecil Balmond, Adjaye developed and installed a vaulting system that, due to the weight and complicated nature of *Afro Kaleidoscope*, required slotting a new building within the existing neoclassical one. The final result was an awe-inspiring oculus that dramatically erupted a fractal pattern from the painting, expanding it outward.

Even before *Within Reach*, Adjaye had begun designing his colored-glass Idea Store libraries in London (2004 and 2005; page 208), for which he developed glass cladding systems. The timing of *Within Reach* was fortuitous. Later, taking these studies to the extreme, Adjaye applied similar logic to the colossal Moscow School of Management, SKOLKOVO (2010; page 230). His collaborations with Ofili continued, too—next, with a laminated scrim for the Stephen Lawrence Center in London (2007; page 214) and, after that, with Hill House (2015), a concrete home and studio perched on the hills of Port of Spain, Trinidad and Tobago. In 2019, Adjaye again returned to the Venice Biennale, this time as the architect of the first-ever Ghana Pavilion, for which he designed an exhibition titled *Ghana Freedom*.

Picking up the red, black, and green hues from Chris Ofili's paintings referencing the pan-African union flag, Adjaye's 2003 British Pavilion glass ceiling sculpture, *Afro Kaleidoscope*, refracted the light through an array of sharp, contrasting colors, creating a sense of ethereality.

Soft, muted carpeting and the monochromatic palette of each room created an immersive viewing experience.

Each interior gallery was enveloped in a single color, dissolving the materiality of the walls, floor, and ceiling.

Bold, vibrant hues from Ofili's paintings were amplified through saturating the rooms with them—absorbing the visitor into meditative, color-washed encounters.

Becoming the pavilion's central skylight, *Afro Kaleidoscope* was suspended from the ceiling and echoed the vibrant tapestry of colors that defined the interior galleries.

The thresholds between rooms were geometrically distorted and thickened, powerfully framing the paintings on display.

Idea Stores/Chrisp Street & Whitechapel Road London, UK, 2004 and 2005

A major breakthrough for Adjaye, the Idea Stores were his first two public buildings, his first competition win, and an early foreshadowing of his rare ability to establish a profound presence through community-oriented architecture. Both projects could be viewed as thresholds, literal and figurative, for the then emerging architect, and for the communities they serve. Commissioned by the London Borough of Tower Hamlets as a way to rethink the library in the twenty-first century—by making informational and educational facilities more accessible and widely usable—the Idea Stores reflect their unusual name: both are located in retail settings and take cues from their surroundings. Wrapped in vertically arranged glass bars that allude to the striped awning material of the district's market stalls, they feature exterior glass panels tinted in five shades of green and five of blue, with clear glass mixed in.

Although both employ the same glazing system, the buildings use their glass facades to different effect: the first structure, on Chrisp Street, is constructed with steel-framed timber supports, and at 14,760 square feet (1,270 square meters) is much more condensed, the bulk of it situated atop ground-level shopfronts; its exterior emphasizes the stretched-out length of its east-facing side. The second Idea Store, next to a busy street market on the north side of Whitechapel Road, is a self-bracing building framed in concrete; its facade highlights its five-story height and 37,000-square-foot (3,440-square-meter) heft. Inside both, Adjaye mixes rough, plain materials, emphasizing each in contrast with the other: rubber floors (green at Chrisp, red at Whitechapel), steel staircases, rows of floor-to-ceiling laminated veneer lumber fins, custom spruce plywood furniture and shelving, exposed-beam ceilings, and suspended zigzag strip lights.

At both locations, escalators lead visitors up from street-level entrances. Whitechapel's ground-floor escalator, situated underneath a front facade that cantilevers out and covers a second, internal glass wall, lands directly on the sidewalk—a barrier-free portal from city to library, and a means to draw street life in. (The resulting atrium features vents that automatically open to avoid overheating in the summer.) Through its material and form, the indoor–outdoor space at Whitechapel creates a compressed chasm of light—during the day, it harnesses sunlight; at night, it becomes a glowing lantern. At once warm and inviting, subtle and sleek—and managing to integrate themselves into the existing urban fabric, despite their different contexts—both projects serve as luminous landmarks.

Top: The Idea Store, Chrisp Street. *Bottom*: The Idea Store, Whitechapel Road. Both projects respond to the materiality and color palette of the streetscape and surroundings.

The colorful facade of the Chrisp Street location touches the street level, providing a playful backdrop to the community's commercial hub.

Inspired by green and blue-striped market stalls, the Whitechapel Road location embraces the vibrancy of the local community.

Above the entrance, warm wooden fins—enclosing windows tinted in a rhythm of color—frame public life; an escalator practically whisks visitors right off the street.

Top: Red rubber flooring contrasts the tinted windows. The quality of light and extensive use of timber create a warm and inviting interior. *Bottom*: The green and blue glass panels are anchored to interior timber fins.

Stephen Lawrence Center London, UK, 2007

Adjaye's first memorial project—and a notable predecessor to the Gwangju Reading Room (2013; page 184) in South Korea, the Smithsonian National Museum of African American History and Culture (2016; page 142) in Washington, DC, and the Cherry Groce Memorial Pavilion (2021) in London—the Stephen Lawrence Center was created in memory of an 18-year-old Black architecture student who was murdered at a southeast London bus stop by a group of white racists in 1993. Commissioned by the Stephen Lawrence Trust, a diversity, equity, and inclusion organization founded in 1998 that invests in underserved young people and helps train them for creative professions, the 4,330-square-foot (1,320-square-meter) center comprises two triangular pavilions with educational spaces, computer suites, offices, and exhibition galleries.

Located along the west bank of the Ravensbourne River in London's Deptford neighborhood, the site was previously owned by a water company and features an existing network of zigzagging underground pipes. Designed to allow for emergency below-ground access and to accommodate the pipework, Adjaye's jagged structure also responds to and engages with the river, nearby roads, and the mix of surrounding residential buildings. Clad in glass and perforated steel, it is a porous building that manages to both stand out from and blend into its surroundings—a bold architectural tribute to Lawrence and a pragmatically designed community center in one. The structure carries both local and global meaning: one initial reference point for the project was a pair of centuries-old gold boxes from Ghana.

The project's focal point, a collaboration with the artist Chris Ofili, is its two-story, 40-foot-wide (12.2-meter) floor-to-ceiling glass screen with a moiré pattern by Ofili printed on reflective laminated film. In the late afternoon sun, the entry foyer transforms as Ofili's monumental work hits the room's illuminated red wall, becoming all at once a neighborhood reminder, a signifier of the brutality that took place, a reflection of a youth's life lost, and a subtle symbolic reference to activist Marcus Garvey's notion of "Black blood." Ofili's geometric veil adds even greater meaning and depth, its fractal shadows emblematic of water washing over a blood-red space. These combined, the room becomes an artistic and architectural form of redemption.

The use of metal mesh as a cladding material amplifies the dappled sunlight that streams through the trees in the adjacent park.

Top: Based upon a drawing by Chris Ofili, the moiré pattern on the lower half of the main entrance facade is printed on a reflective film and laminated between two panels of glass.
Bottom: The screen-patterned windows, as seen from the interior lobby.

Natural light enters the community center through playful apertures in the walls and ceiling. *Following spread*: The lobby lights up a bright red color at night, a not-so-subtle reference to Marcus Garvey's notion of "Black blood."

Museum of Contemporary Art Denver
Denver, CO, US, 2007

Adjaye's first public building in the United States and his first-ever museum project, the Museum of Contemporary Art Denver (MCA) was a profound testing ground for the architect, a study for how to bring light, both soft and direct, into space. Thinking about the city's mile-high altitude and its proximity to the sun—Denver is one of the sunniest cities in America—Adjaye and his team analyzed around twenty years' worth of local sunlight data to understand the sun's movement and intensity, and designed the four-story, nearly 25,000-square-foot (2,320-square-meter) building partly in relation to those patterns. As with the Idea Stores (2004 and 2005; page 208) in London, the cubelike MCA was made to be a reflector and refractor throughout the day and a lantern at night. With its monochromatic material palette, the building allows natural light to gently permeate its interior. During the day, a T-shaped roof light washes the atrium in light, while a multilayered facade system creates an ethereal interior glow, particularly on the second floor, which features three galleries organized as freestanding volumes wrapped by a circulation spine. The building's shell consists of an amalgamation of glazing materials: a double-glass panel with a gray-tinted window on the outside and a clear one on the inside, both with sandblasted inner faces, and an insulation layer of Monopan, a translucent plastic, sandwiched in between.

Arranged in three separate stacks, the building's gallery spaces accommodate a wide range of programming, allowing them to be used separately or in combination. The structure also includes education and lecture rooms, offices, a bookshop, and a rooftop garden and glass-box café. Throughout, Adjaye devised a series of transitional moments that serve as architectural punctuation marks, providing views of the city and brief visual breaks in between the galleries.

Various other materials add to the tactile navigational experience: gray-stained American redwood cladding is applied at the ground-floor entrance vestibule and on the roof, while steel is used for a central staircase, landings, and railings, and concrete for the floors. To the west, across an alleyway, sits Adjaye's slim-lined LN House (2008), a private residence covered in Cor-Ten steel, which, despite its stark material contrast to the museum's glassy exterior, appears as a sort of sibling to the MCA; to the east, MCA's angled facade opens up to 15th Street, with aperture views looking out toward downtown Denver.

The museum's exterior interacts with sunlight through the layering of monochromatic materials of varying opacities—a double-glazed panel with gray-tinted glass on the outside and clear glass on the inside. The inner faces of both are sandblasted, diffusing daylight on the interior to protect the collections and give off a warm, glowing effect.

At night, the museum becomes a sort of lantern. A play between completely translucent and opaque glazing opens up views of the interior.

The use of glass on the floor, wall, and ceiling of the building, shown here on the rooftop terrace, subtly reflects the ephemeral nature of the museum as a non-collecting institution and its temporary exhibitions.

A glass walkway on the roof doubles as a skylight, diffusing light deep into the white-walled interiors.

The museum's central staircase, made of steel, creates reverberating sounds when visitors walk up and down it between floors.

A wood-clad box that cantilevers off the glazed facade asserts a strong presence from afar, becoming less pronounced as visitors approach the building.

Apertures blur boundaries between indoors and out, and between the museum complex and the surrounding city. *Following spread*: The building was designed to fit both the needs of the institution and its narrow site, which runs along 15th Street. Adjaye's LN House (2008) is next door, separated by an alleyway.

ALWAYS SOMETHING NEW
YU-CHENG CHOU
TIM NOBLE & SUE WEBSTER
TUESDAY-SUNDAY 10AM-6PM
EVERY FRIDAY UNTIL 10PM
MCA DENVER
1485

Moscow School of Management, SKOLKOVO Moscow, RU, 2010

A nine-story, roughly 460,000-square-foot (43,000-square-meter) curvilinear megastructure, the Moscow School of Management, SKOLKOVO, with its delicate design and layout, belies its gargantuan size. Through its expansive, disc-shaped concrete base and sandblasted glass facade (which cleverly plays with opacity and reflection), Adjaye designed a sculptural, citadel-like centerpiece for a campus to come. Prior to the project, most of Adjaye's work had been, by comparison, small-scale and located in dense urban cores—projects that were his humble way of adding to or suturing the city. With SKOLKOVO, he was, in effect, hired to make the city.

Topped with four jutting cantilevers in varying sizes, each clad in patterned, colored aluminum-composite panels, the building is similar to an international airport terminal in scale, yet, because of its abstracted form and glass-aluminum interplay, it somehow manages to sit sensitively within the surrounding landscape. A postmodernist design, SKOLVOVO is literally and figuratively a global construction: the building's patterns and form embrace both Yoruba culture—a reference Adjaye later nodded to in the tiered crown of the Smithsonian National Museum of African American History and Culture (2016; page 142) in Washington, DC—and Russian Constructivism, namely the work of 1920s avant-garde architect Konstantin Melnikov. Using computer-imaging software, Adjaye and his team devised seven pixelated, light-inspired patterns with which he clad the building. Inside the sprawling space are lecture halls, a cafeteria, residential spaces, a 660-seat auditorium, a 126-room hotel, basketball courts, a fitness center, and an Olympic-size swimming pool.

More than anything, Adjaye wanted SKOLKOVO to provide a way of orienting oneself. The building, in essence, is architecture as compass and clock: organized around the rotation of the sun, it is a circular, glass-walled embodiment of Adjaye's obsession with perching and observing. Morning spaces face east, toward dawn; afternoon and evening spaces west, toward dusk. Various spectral effects intentionally shift hour to hour, day to day, month to month, season to season. Eschewing the concept of a traditional Oxbridge-style quad, Adjaye instead created a single structure comprising easily identifiable volumes—a climatically responsive terrain in and of itself, built for six-month-long winters. The result is a new architectural "condition" not to do with the city at all, but with a building's relationship to nature.

Situated in a wooded valley near Moscow, the structure features four patterned glass masses that cantilever off a two-story, disc-shaped building.

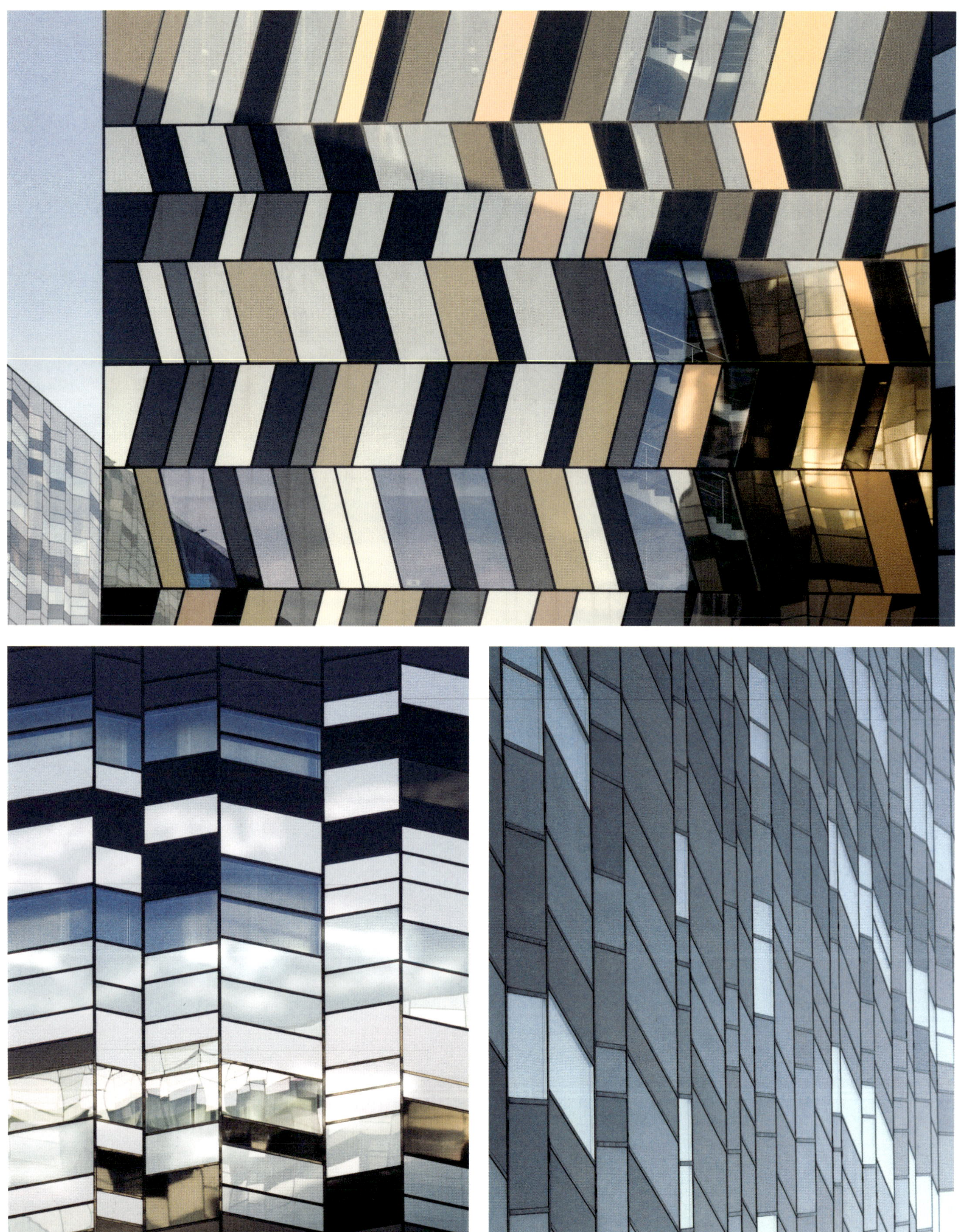

The facade of the four rectangular masses is composed of colorful glass in a herringbone pattern, bonded with aluminum composite panels.

The interior design echoes the rhythmic exterior fins that wrap the structure's central disk. Within this monochromatic space, colored glass is used to draw the visitor deeper into the building, seen here with a stairway's blue glass balustrade. *Following spead*: The inside of the gymnasium reveals how the slanted glass openings play with light.

Previous spread: The massive building, as seen in the winter, with its dramatic, jutting rectangular blocks atop a central disc. *Above*: The form of the campus, inspired by the art of the Russian Constructivist Kazimir Malevich, features color-blocked geometric shapes.

To accommodate long, cold Russian winters, the complex was conceived as a single development with clearly identifiable volumes, allowing for a full-functioning year-round environment.

Francis A. Gregory Neighborhood Library Washington, DC, US, 2012

Situated on the edge of Fort Davis Park in southeastern Washington, DC, the shimmering Francis A. Gregory Library welcomes in, reflects back, and extends out toward its woodland surroundings. Conceptually linked to the twin Idea Stores (2004 and 2005; page 208) in London and created as a sibling of the nearby William O. Lockridge/Bellevue Library (2012; page 174), the two-story, 23,000-square-foot (2,140-square-meter) Gregory Library features a steel-frame structure that is enclosed in a facade of diamond-shaped glass panels. Twenty-four feet (7.3 meters) in height, the pavilion-style building is covered in a louvered, cantilevering steel canopy—not unlike that of Mies van der Rohe's 1968 Neue Nationalgalerie in Berlin—that forms a quietly assertive, hovering presence. Drawing the eyes in, the roof overhang also provides an inviting entryway and a sunshade.

Inspired in part by the work of Ron Eglash, an ethno-mathematician who has studied fractal patterns throughout Indigenous African design practices, as well as by 1970s optical art, such as the kinetic works of the artist Len Lye, Adjaye applied the notion of a fractal as an architectural organizing device. Using parametric tools, the architect scaled the monolithic volume in a glass exterior of panels in varying widths, from 5 to 11 feet (1.5 to 3.3 meters), so that each is slightly different in size. Materials are carefully choreographed throughout, emphasizing the building's indoor–outdoor relationship. Inside, interlocking stained plywood modules dance in lockstep with the outside glass panels, which alternate between clear and mirror-finished panes, creating a dramatic shadow effect. Natural light also enters through the suspended glass-clad ceiling of the library's double-height atrium, with diamond-shaped panels on the roof adding another visual layer.

Comprising designated spaces for adults, teenagers, and children, as well as a public meeting room and conference rooms, the library features a central black staircase that cuts through the space; pink and green accents provide further orientation cues. An elevated, uplifting environment in more ways than one, the Gregory Library provides a luminous setting designed to heighten awareness—to both what's inside and around it.

Inspired by fractal patterns, the exterior of the library uses geometric progressions made of glass, reflecting the wooded surroundings and adjacent park.

The use of reflective glazing extends the structure outward, suspending it between foliage and sky.

A metal canopy floats above the building, providing a welcoming entrance. *Following spread*: Mirroring the exterior walls, the canopy continues the same diamond pattern, with steel louvers providing moments of shade and dappled sunlight.

Deep-set wood window frames enable seating within the apertures while also framing the outside surroundings in an optical effect.

The geometric structural systems are articulated in the facade, ceiling, and canopy, creating layers through which natural light falls into the library and produces a mosaic of shadows.

The exterior of the building reflects the dense forest that surrounds the far end of the library.

Rammed Earth

Asaase I and *Asaase II* at Gagosian
New York, NY, US
& London, UK, 2021

Dot.Atelier Gallery
Accra, GH, 2023

Shippon Place
Accra, GH, 2023

For Adjaye, rammed earth is a tool of "radical sustainability," a pushback against certain carbon-intensive construction methods, and a philosophical base for re-looking at architecture from Africa. Through his use of the material, Adjaye seeks to forge deep connections between people and the planet. Beyond rammed earth's emotional appeal and tactile qualities, he's particularly attracted to its literal groundedness, as well as its strength and durability; its thermal and acoustic properties; its abundance; and its inherent ecological, low-waste nature. He also views the material as a humanizing means to engage and emphasize localized production, craft, and handwork: rammed earth is made by either manually or mechanically compressing slightly damp soil within a wood or metal frame. Highlighting not only the architect's hand, but also the skill of those that "ram" and make these structures, Adjaye's rammed-earth constructions are physical embodiments of human energy and deep time.

The architect's evolution to working with rammed earth has been long, considered, and osmosis-like. In many respects, it could be considered full circle—a homecoming. Rooted in one of his earliest projects, the reddish-brown Concrete Garden (2001) in London, his more recent turn to the material also stems from several other of his earth-toned, pigmented concrete designs, from his Nkron villa (2012) in Gomoa Fetteh, Ghana; to the McCarter Switching Station (2018) in Newark, New Jersey; to the Winter Park Library (2021) in Florida. It also connects to his ongoing interest in, and studies of, sustainable and long-lasting materials. What ultimately shifted Adjaye's focus toward rammed earth was his family's return to Africa—his primary base since 2019—and his immersion in the city of Accra, where the construction industry has become, in his words, "basically co-opted by Western manufacturing processes."

Embracing raw earth, or what he calls "the most rejected material in the landscape," Adjaye continues to research ancient building techniques, traditional ecological knowledge, and African vernacular designs. (Earth architecture dates back thousands of years, to the Neolithic period.) Looking at its many historical applications, Adjaye finds particular insight in the buildings of Hassan Fathy, a pioneering Egyptian architect known for his use of adobe and traditional mud construction. Within his first two years back in Ghana, Adjaye began creating brick prototypes, clay tiles, structural mock-ups, and cladding systems out of the material. Eventually, with his two respective *Asaase* sculptures (2021) shown at Gagosian in New York and London, he made art installations from locally sourced dirt. He also began work on several rammed-earth structures across Africa, including two that neared completion just as this book was going to print: the Dot.Atelier Gallery (2023) and the cantilevered Shippon Place (2023), both in Accra. Adjaye's future rammed-earth projects include the Thabo Mbeki Presidential Library in Johannesburg, South Africa, an eight-domed, 58,100-square-foot (5,400-square-meter) structure designed to evoke traditional African granaries, which will feature a research center and a museum; a walled-in office compound located next to Accra's Kotoka International Airport; and a prototype for single-story district hospitals across Ghana.

As pragmatic and sustainable as it is symbolic, rammed earth may appear primitive and primordial on the surface, but, as Adjaye's new body of work illustrates, its future potential, when scaled up, could be vast and all-encompassing.

Asaase I and *Asaase II* at Gagosian New York, NY, US & London, UK, 2021

Commissioned for *Social Works*, a two-part group exhibition at Gagosian—organized by curator Antwaun Sargent and exploring the notion of "social space" through works by Black artists—Adjaye created two rammed-earth sculptures. Both titled *Asaase*, a Twi word that translates as "earth," each piece is a potent artwork in its own right and effectively a high-craft material study, an evocative early preview of the architect's larger rammed-earth projects to come.

For the first presentation, shown in New York from June through September 2021, Adjaye made his first-ever large-scale sculpture: a circular, temple-like form comprising sixty tons of crushed earth, sourced from a limestone quarry near Albany, New York, and pounded into rounded, stackable blocks. (A small amount of cement was added for structural support.) Loosely referencing the Tiébélé royal complex in Burkina Faso and the walled city of Agadez in Niger, it meditates on the history of West African architecture. Pairing a pure, simple material with a pure, simple form to create something profound—in this case, an earthen spiral—Adjaye was also thinking of Walter De Maria's *The New York Earth Room* (1977) and the minimalist land art of Robert Smithson. Merging fragments, literal and figurative, *Asaase I* forms a whole new narrative. An anthropological exercise in art-making, Adjaye describes the piece as "a compression of histories." Hefty in presence, it carries the contemplative aura of a hearth, or even of a memorial. It draws visitors in.

As with his sensorial architecture—which so often manages to practically suspend people in space, subtly nudging them to stop, look, and *feel* where they are—here Adjaye created a cavernous coil that invites people to not just turn inward, but to enter it and physically go inward. A layered maze, *Asaase I* opens and closes at various points, creating a disorienting, hypnotic feeling. From the outside, the sculpture's central, chimney-esque column looks solid, but is in fact a void.

With *Asaase II*, exhibited in London from October through December 2021, Adjaye devised an even simpler structure: four rammed-earth beams, made of British laterite soil, that call to mind a termite mound.

Previous spread and *above*: Referencing historic West African architecture, *Asaase I*, shown here in 2021 at Gagosian's gallery in New York's Chelsea neighborhood, serves as a sort of modern-day relic, offering a shifting sequence of compression and expansion.

Composed of curved fragments and chambers, the sculpture invites people to meander through its observatory-like enclosure.

The totemic *Asaase II*, shown here in 2021 at Gagosian gallery in London, meditates on the relationship between the human body and fragments of earth.

The texture of the sculpture's horizontal lines resembles the "horizons" within a cross-section of soil and materializes geometric forms.

Dot.Atelier Gallery
Accra, GH, 2023

When Adjaye was approached to design a home, studio, and gallery complex for the Ghanaian painter Amoako Boafo, he thought back to one of his earliest building projects: the streetscape-defining Dirty House in London's Shoreditch neighborhood (2002; page 34), originally conceived for the artists Sue Webster and Tim Noble. Located near the Accra waterfront (and a short distance from the Sandbox Complex, a beach club Adjaye designed in 2020), the Dot.Atelier Gallery sits within an area that Adjaye views as a "little Venice," referring to the bohemian, bungalow-filled California beach town. Near where his civil servant turned diplomat father, Affram, lived after he moved to the capital from his small village in the Akuapem Hills of Ghana, the project is, for Adjaye, deeply personal and a way of "trying to sense the presence of my father." A homecoming of sorts, it is an architectural form of ancestral recall.

Considering the project at once a "manifesto," an "exercise," and his "Dirty House for Accra," Adjaye hopes the gallery and studio will ignite an alternative way of developing urban projects—one that's much less toxic and more African, or local, in terms of material sourcing. Designed for the modern-day city but with ancient dwellings in mind, this is no mere craft test; rather, it's Adjaye's way of transforming a dense site and its surroundings through the creation of a subtle but potent architectural aura. Following not only Dirty House, but also projects such as Pitch Black, in Brooklyn—built for the artists Lorna Simpson and James Casebere, and completed in 2006—and Mole House (2019; page 74) in London, for Sue Webster, Dot.Atelier Gallery is yet another artist space designed by Adjaye that serves as a beacon, an architectural tool for rethinking a neighborhood.

The first of two adjacent "twin" buildings, this monolithic structure features a three-story gallery and studio, a café, a retail space, a library, an office, and an external generator yard at the front of the site. A second building, to come next door, will include an artist residency space and a home. Following what Adjaye calls an "Earth neighborhood" thesis, the project embodies his belief that, if expanded, rammed-earth architecture—beyond being healthy for human habitation and ecologically sensitive—could become a natural carbon sink.

The monolithic building comprises three stacked volumes—broken up visually by concrete bands—that gradually expand in height to accommodate the gallery's public and artist-residency programs.

A double-envelope facade encloses an internal “circulation spine” extending from the ground level to the top floor.

Top: Large windows are shaded by the building's two-layer skin, prioritizing unobstructed views and optimal thermal qualities. *Bottom*: Each level features apertures that frame views of both the ocean and the immediate urban context, maintaining visual connections to Accra's emerging waterfront neighborhood.

Previous spread: Referencing the angled roofs of neighboring structures, the top-floor gallery level is defined by a sawtooth roof that bathes the space in natural diffused light. *Above*: The interior features rammed-earth walls that provide a material link between inside and outdoors.

Sculpted openings on the ground floor look out on the landscaped garden that surrounds the squat rectangular structure.

Shippon Place
Accra, GH, 2023

Located in the residential neighborhood of Cantonments, Shippon Place was designed to look and feel more like a house than an office building. Even with its long, rectangular form and material heft, the three-level structure manages to maintain an intimate presence. Its exposed double-height volume and 82-foot-long (26-meter) cantilevering slab practically float above the street level. Adjaye's intent? To build a sort of twenty-first-century Miesien courtyard structure that befits its surroundings, but also forms a pronounced presence.

A contemporary take on an *impluvium*—the sunken part of a house's atrium in early Roman and Greek architecture, designed to receive rainwater and carry it away—Shippon Place features a concrete foundation and support columns, a steel frame, and rammed-earth tiles for its facade and roof cladding. A high-tech structure, paired with what Adjaye calls an "earthbound architecture system," the building merges typologies and references from across time to form a new building prototype. Viewing Shippon Place as a "wellness space," Adjaye sought to highlight the landscape around it, integrating the site's sloping topography and forging an inside–outside relationship between building and garden. Made of yellowish rammed-earth tiles that the architect devised with a local production plant, the structure's elegant facade frames views of the cityscape, bringing the outdoors in through a *shakkei* effect, in a way that's similar to Adjaye's timber-finned William O. Lockridge Library (2012; page 174) in Washington, DC. Inside, the fins moderate the climate, creating ever-shifting shadows and pools of light.

In addition to office spaces, the building includes a conference room and a rooftop lounge and bar with a pergola. Beyond an external guardhouse at the front of the site, there's a *porte-cochère*, where cars can pull directly up to the ground-level reception area. In a classic Adjaye duality—one that goes all the way back to Elektra House (1999) in London—on the outside, the structure appears monolithic and weighty; inside, timber paneling, exposed steel frames, and rammed-earth walls form a space of lightness and luminosity.

Appearing to balance on a single monolithic column, the structure comprises an 85-foot (26-meter) cantilevered slab of rammed earth tiles suspended over a parking area. *Following spread*: Rammed-earth fins on the exterior extend inward, both creating a rhythmic presence from the street and framing views of the city from within.

Previous spread: The building's rammed-earth panels speak to the artisanal approach of the construction, as well as to the human energy that built it. *Above*: The ombré tones and textures of the fins have an earthen quality that naturally integrates the building within the surrounding land, trees, and sky.

Inside, light passes through the fins, illuminating a rammed-earth wall that defines the in-between circulation spaces of the second floor.

Afterword
Spencer Bailey

> Writing is a way to salvage life, to give it form and meaning. It exposes what we have hidden, unearths what we have neglected, misremembered, denied. It is a method of capturing, of pinning down, but it is also a form of truth, of liberation.
> —Jhumpa Lahiri[1]

Architecture, as with writing, is at its heart sensemaking. Architecture can indeed be seen as its own "written" form of communication. Of visioning, of marking, of calibration, of translation, of melding and reconfiguring language—*materials*—to create a kind of magic. To forge, through radical material mutations, what David Adjaye calls "alchemy." Similar to an unforgettable novel, a building can coalesce in such a way, fusing together its many components and parts, so as to activate a heightened atmosphere and evoke a particularly strong aura and energy. In our postcolonial, postindustrial, hyper-streamlined Anthropocene age of efficiency, as with storytelling, architecture has the special ability, when properly harnessed, to transfigure how one sees the world, to bring about memories of—and form essential links to—cultures, climates, and geographies.

Adjaye's practice began in London, in the mid-1990s, through an exploration of elemental materials, usually in their primary state. In many respects reflections on trauma and hope, his early buildings were built to be, just as they are today, spaces that elevate whomever comes in contact with them, and that respond to—and counter the onslaught of—the banal globalized architectural homogeneity that has become all too common now in cities around the world. Starting with the Idea Stores (2004 and 2005) in London, Adjaye's work has become more and more public- and community-oriented over time.

Throughout, he has sought to create platforms of potential: environments that shape new behaviors and create new opportunities.

Adjaye continues in this tradition today, but expansively so. With his main base in Accra since 2019, he increasingly makes buildings that serve as philosophical starting points for re-looking at the world—largely from an African perspective. By turning to ancient African, Indigenous, and near-ancestral wisdom and centuries-old building techniques, technologies, and traditions, then repositioning them in a language of the now, using today's tools, Adjaye is providing literal, physical spaces from which to reconsider the continent—its histories, its cultures, its peoples, its geographies, its *architecture*—and the planet anew.

Deeply rooted acknowledgments that past histories can't be divorced from the present, Adjaye's buildings reflect on what the writer Saidiya Hartman has referred to as "temporal entanglement, where the past, the present, and the future are not discrete and cut off from one another."[2] Providing new codes through which to understand, experience, and navigate the world, Adjaye's structures are space-time positioning devices. They respect and reflect on the past with an eye toward the future, firmly planting those who interact with them in the here and now.

Adjaye's is an expansive architecture—of cosmology, of universality, of liberation. It is imbued with meaning and feeling. It anchors people and helps them make sense of their lives. It is, by extension, an architecture of "subversive historiography" as defined by the late author and activist bell hooks. "Subversive historiography," she writes, "connects oppositional practices from the past with forms of resistance in the present, thus creating spaces of possibility where the future can be imagined differently—imagined in such a way that we can witness ourselves dreaming, moving forward and beyond the limits and confines of fixed locations."[3]

Through his work, Adjaye also embraces what the philosopher and social critic Cornel West refers to, in his 1993 essay "Race and Architecture," as a "new architectural historiography," one that requires "its conception of the 'past' and 'present' be attuned to the complex role of difference—nature, primitive, ruled, Dionysian, female, Black, and so on."[4] West asks, "Where do we go from here?"[5] Over the past three decades, Adjaye's buildings—from Dirty House (2002) in London; to the Smithsonian National Museum of African American History and Culture (2016) in Washington, DC; to the Dot.Atelier Gallery (2023) in Accra—have shown the way, proving to be such architectural North Stars, bold and needed answers to our complex present and future.

In many respects, Adjaye's agenda is one of decolonization, his humble way of re-*righting* history. From Elektra House (1999) on, practically every one of his projects, in one way or another, subtly or not, has been built in resistance to what he describes as "the standardization of the colonial project." Through both "material imagination," to use a term coined by the French philosopher Gaston Bachelard,[6] and "prophetic aesthetics" (cultural critic B. Ruby Rich's phrase),[7] Adjaye brings with him an arsenal of material know-how, specificity, and *presence* to all that he does—his pushback against the soul-numbing, cheaply and quickly built non-spaces that have been foisted upon the world by colonization and through sped-up Western manufacturing processes.

Now, as countries across the African continent continue to grapple with the residue of colonialism and the afterlife of the transatlantic slave trade, Adjaye sees a profound opportunity forward through the construction industry: to bring back—to unearth, even—ancient techniques, and to pair them with modern technologies and engineering. Just as languages used in government and media in Africa largely remain those that were once imposed by a colonial power, much of the continent's architecture remains linked to its colonial past. By embracing certain earthly materials—mud, timber, stone—Adjaye seeks to form a new polyvocal future, with new polyvocal narratives.

In his book *In the Break: The Aesthetics of the Black Radical Tradition*, the poet and theorist Fred Moten opens with the line, "The history of Blackness is testament to the fact that objects can and do resist."[8] Adjaye's buildings, in their own way, do exactly that. They are of this Black radical tradition. They *resist*. They're visceral. They're felt. They sing. They invoke what Moten calls a "a kind of lyricism of the surplus—invagination, rupture, collision, augmentation."[9] As with the blues—which, in historian and writer Jelani Cobb's words, "exist for the express purpose of alchemizing beauty from pain"[10]—Adjaye's architecture can be viewed as a vocal form of expression, rich in narrative and powerfully conveyed.

Transcendent and metamorphic, Adjaye's structures also evince what West, in his 1996 essay "Black Strivings in a Twilight Civilization," calls the "*ur*-text of Black culture:" "a guttural cry and a wrenching moan—a cry not so much for help as for home, a moan less out of complaint than for *recognition*." West writes:

> The most profound Black cultural products—John Coltrane's saxophone solos, James Cleveland's gut gospels, Billie Holiday's vocal leaps, Rev. Gardner Taylor's rhapsodic sermons, James Baldwin's poignant essays, Alvin Ailey's graceful dances, Toni Morrison's dissonant novels—transform and transfigure in artistic form this cry and moan.[11]

Vocal leaps, poignant essays, and graceful dances in their own rights, Adjaye's ethereal spaces share these sensibilities. Each of his projects is, as the poet, essayist, and playwright Elizabeth Alexander has written of Coltrane's *A Love Supreme*, its very own form of Black chant—a chant, she writes, that "sustains us. It is balm. It is remembrance. It is provocation. It is incantation. It is human. It is power."[12] This chant is felt across all of Adjaye's output: at the Stephen Lawrence Center (2007) in London, at the Piety Bridge and Wharf (2014) in New Orleans, at the Sugar Hill mixed-use development (2015) in

Harlem, at the 130 William skyscraper (2021) in downtown Manhattan, at the Winter Park Library (2021) in Florida. It is a chant expressed perhaps no more powerfully than on the National Mall at the NMAAHC.

Adjaye's approach, as it has been since he was a master's student at the Royal College of Art in the early 1990s, is also, importantly, about appreciating and understanding the power of the earth, the human relationship to it, and our evolution *with* it, all subjects key to addressing today's climate crisis. For Adjaye, architecture is a means of interfacing with nature through the creation of what he calls a "new artifice." Thinking all the way back to the Neolithic Revolution of 10,000 BCE, during which humans shifted from hunting and gathering to agriculture and settlement, the architect sees his work in a thousands-of-years-long continuum of humans reconstituting the earth. As is evidenced through his deep, ongoing research into ancient forms and African vernacular architecture, Adjaye views his buildings as subversive, cross-generational acts. A counter to conventional carbon-intensive constructions, his more recent rammed-earth projects in particular are built as structures of resistance and resilience, a means of ecological and social power in the face of climate disaster—his pragmatic way of returning to ancient traditions, urgently applied to the now.

Through colonialism and colonization, Western architectural orders took over in the seventeenth, eighteenth, and nineteenth centuries. Traditional construction techniques using raw earth, the most abundant material on the planet, were pushed to the side by ascendant powers, who in turn inserted European styles, built structures with industrialized materials, and made them dominant. In the twentieth century, this continued, but in the Modernist mode. Across the centuries, colonizing architectural agendas were imposed on landscapes and cityscapes. Architecture became a key tool with which to emphasize and even dictate supremacy. Entire ways of building and living were bulldozed. Today, much traditional ecological knowledge around building from raw earth remains lost, or at the very least underexplored and unutilized. Jean Dethier, an expert on raw-earth architecture, calls the current situation "a deep-rooted cultural neglect, a form of collective amnesia," and notes that "raw-earth construction has long been an unacknowledged means of democratization."[13]

With this history in mind, Adjaye considers rammed-earth architecture a crucial method for building away from discord and toward balance and oneness. For him, working with rammed earth presents a metaphysical opportunity, an essential way of looking at, working with, and being *of* the earth—of collectively being more in touch with the world around us, each other, and ourselves. It's a sentiment Dethier echoes: "This architecture has the potential to be part of the global paradigm shift that our society urgently requires if its future survival is to be ensured. This radical change, philosophical and moral as well as technological and political, is needed to free the construction sector from the grip of the technoscience that threatens to overwhelm us."[14]

Through sheer determination, clear-eyed vision, and extraordinary execution, from offices in Accra, London, and New York, Adjaye continues to realize his alchemical approach to architecture, with increased velocity and impact, across a wide range of scales and typologies, from his sculptural *Assase* installations at Gagosian (2021) in New York and London; to the Abrahamic Family House interfaith complex (2023) in Abu Dhabi; to several landmark megaprojects currently underway, including the Thabo Mbeki Presidential Library in South Africa; the National Cathedral of Ghana in Accra; and the Edo Museum of West African Art in Benin City, Nigeria. Nearly thirty years into his practice, Adjaye has built a formidable firm that has the power and potential to bring more and more of this thinking to bear on a global scale. To create spaces of prayer and grace, of collectivity and *connectivity*—and of pause. Spaces that allow for deeper readings and fuller meanings; that bring about slower, more considered ways of being, thinking, and feeling; and that activate one's sense of aliveness and worth.

What Adjaye's great body of work reveals and represents—*writes*—is transformative change. It is a hopeful horizon.

1
Jhumpa Lahiri, *Translating Myself and Others* (2022), Princeton University Press, 31.

2
Thora Siemsen, "On working with archives: An interview with writer Saidiya Hartman," April 18, 2018, The Creative Independent, thecreativeindependent.com/people/saidiya-hartman-on-working-with-archives

3
bell hooks, "Black Vernacular: Architecture as Cultural Practice," *Art on My Mind: Visual Politics* (1995), The New Press, 151.

4
Cornel West, *The Cornel West Reader* (1999), Basic Civitas Books, 460.

5
West, *The Cornel West Reader*, 462.

6
Nathaniel Coleman, *Materials and Meaning in Architecture: Essays on the Bodily Experience of Buildings* (2020), Bloomsbury, 4.

7
bell hooks, "Architecture in Black Life: Talking Space With LaVerne Wells-Bowie," *Art on My Mind: Visual Politics* (1995), The New Press, 159.

8
Fred Moten, *In the Break: The Aesthetics of the Black Radical Tradition* (2003), University of Minnesota Press, 1.

9
Moten, *In the Break*, 26.

10
Jelani Cobb, *The Devil & Dave Chappelle: And Other Essays* (2007), Thunder's Mouth Press, 157.

11
West, *The Cornel West Reader*, 102.

12
Elizabeth Alexander, *The Trayvon Generation* (2022), Grand Central Publishing, 125.

13
Jean Dethier, *The Art of Earth Architecture* (2020), Princeton Architectural Press, 8.

14
Dethier, *The Art of Earth Architecture*, 12.

Credits

Courtesy of Adjaye Associates: Cover image (top left), 16 (top and bottom), 23, 48 (top and bottom), 84 (bottom, left), 191, 194–95, 196213 (bottom)

Courtesy of Aishti Foundation: 137 (top)

David Alf: 84 (bottom right), 243

Emeline Allemand: 35 (bottom)

Courtesy of American Hardwood Export Council: 171

Aram Arakelyan: 231

Courtesy of The Aram Gallery: 18

Courtesy of Art Institute of Chicago: 160 (bottom)

Spencer Bailey: 14

© Dror Baldinger, FAIA: 65, 66 (top right), 67 (bottom left), 70–71, 72, 73, 85 (top left and right), 89, 90, 91 (top and bottom), 92–93, 96, 97, 103, 104, 105, 106, 110, 254–55, 256, 257

Chad Baumer: 108–9

Cameraphoto Arte: Cover image (bottom left) 202, 203, 204 (top and bottom), 205 (top and bottom), 206, 207

Lyndon Douglas: 13, 20 (top), 36 (left and right), 37 (left and right), 124, 215, 216 (top), 218–19

Denis Esakov: 238

Assen Emilov: 125, 126–27

Courtesy of EskewDumezRipple: 130 (bottom)

Brad Feinknopf: 148

Leonardo Finotti: 167 (bottom), 168–69, 172–73

Leonid Furmansky: 66 (bottom), 69 (top right)

Laurian Ghinitoiu: 81, 82–83, 84 (top), 85 (bottom), 86–87

Tim Hursley: 129, 130 (top), 131, 132–33

Ilya Ivanov: 232 (top, bottom left and right), 239

Charlie Joslin: 66 (top left), 67 (top and bottom right)

Alan Karchmer, courtesy of Smithsonian NMAAHC: Cover image (top right), 147, 149

Ivane Katamashvili: 57, 59 (top left and right), 58, 59 (bottom), 95, 98, 99, 100–101, 107, 111, 143, 152, 244–45, 248

Dean Kaufman: 225

Nic Lehoux: 144 (top and bottom), 145 (top and bottom), 146, 150–51, 223, 224, 227, 228–29

Christian Lohfink: 192, 193

Carlotta Luke: 216 (bottom)

Mark Menjivar: 68, 69 (bottom and top left)

Wilfred Petzi, courtesy of Haus der Kunst: 164–65

Ron Pollard, courtesy MCA Denver: 19 (bottom)

Emily Minton Redfield: 17

Ed Reeve: Cover image (bottom right), 30 (top and bottom), 31, 32 (left and right), 33, 35 (top), 39, 40 (bottom and top), 41, 42 (left and right), 52 (top), 75, 76 (left and right), 77, 78–79, 161 (top), 162, 163, 167 (top), 170, 221, 222, 226, 233, 234–35, 258, 259

Nikolay Sachkov: 236–37

Jeff Sauer: 182–83

Maxine Schnitzer: 175, 177, 246

Kyungsub Shin: 185, 186, 187, 188-89

Tim Soar: 209 (top and bottom), 210, 211, 212, 213 (top)

Edmund Sumner: 176, 178, 179, 180, 181, 217, 241, 242, 247

Jad Sylla: 136 (bottom), 139

Bisher Tabbaa: 49

Edem J. Tamakloe: 262, 263 (top and bottom), 264–65, 266, 267, 269, 270–71, 272–73, 274, 275

James Wang: 19 (top), 20 (middle), 60, 61, 62–63

Jonty Wilde: 158–59, 160 (top), 161 (bottom)

Studio Hans Wilschut: 20 (bottom)

Xia Zhi: 43, 44–45

Guillaume Ziccarelli: 135, 136 (top), 137 (bottom), 138, 140–41

Wade Zimmerman: 47, 50–51, 54–55, 52 (bottom), 53

Index

Page numbers in *italics* refer to illustrations.

Acknowledgments
Spencer Bailey

First and foremost, I'd like to express my deep gratitude to David. Throughout the process of making *Alchemy*, he was incredibly generous with his thoughts and time. Thank you, David.

David and I first met in 2011, shortly after he had completed the Moscow School of Management, SKOLKOVO, in Russia, and I never could have imagined how fortuitous our crossing of paths would be. In large part because of our many intersecting interests, David and I have since forged what I consider to be my longest-running interview: a kaleidoscopic series of conversations, probably numbering around thirty or so and spanning twelve years, about life and death, cities, architecture, landscape, art, light and shadow, the built environment, "luxury," nature, culture, memory and memorials, Japan (particularly Kyoto and the Katsura Imperial Villa), Isamu Noguchi, racial politics, Blackness, the African diaspora, slavery, colonialism, trauma, the climate crisis, materials, and so much else. Extending out of this dialogue, David wrote a beautiful Foreword to my previous book with Phaidon, *In Memory Of: Designing Contemporary Memorials* (2020).

In late 2018, during an interview for *Town & Country* magazine, in Miami's Design District, David mentioned the notion of alchemy to me for the first time, describing how certain material junctions can form "an alchemic power." Almost immediately, I thought, *Alchemy* should be the title of a book about how David chooses, uses, and combines materials, and the extraordinary architecture that results. This is that book.

Extra thanks go to Marissa Glauberman, who shepherded this project every step of the way and helped make it a reality. I couldn't have done this without you.

Thanks, too, to the rest of the Adjaye Associates team: Luisa Alves, for your scheduling prowess; Michael Matey, for organizing the pictures; Eric Ball, Russell Crader, and Glenn DeRoche, for your added perspectives; and Alexandria Galloway. I would also like to thank Josh Ellman, no longer at the firm, with whom I ignited some of the earliest conversations about making a book with David, years before it would morph into this.

Thank you to Teresita Fernández for contributing your thoughtful, evocative Foreword. Your understanding of alchemy is a vital addition to this project.

Thank you to Stellene Volandes and Erik Maza at *Town & Country*. Without that interview for the April 2019 issue, the idea for this book could very well still be floating in the ether. And thank you to Stephen Pulvirent and Jonathan Bues for the *Hodinkee Magazine* assignments on Noguchi's Akari sculptures; Mira Nakashima and the George Nakashima house, studio, and workshop; Eileen Gray's E-1027 house; and the Rothko Chapel restoration and expansion. Each of these furthered my perspective on alchemy as it relates to architecture, art, and design.

Thank you to the writers, journalists, curators, and scholars whose texts about David and his firm's work helped me form the framework for this book, particularly Peter Allison, Okwui Enwezor, Michael Kimmelman, Marc McQuade, Zoë Ryan, Diane Solway, and Calvin Tomkins.

Thank you to those whose writings and/or perspectives (and in certain cases, friendships) have helped provide me with additional insights to this project, in both direct and indirect ways: Paola Antonelli, Glenn Adamson, Elizabeth Alexander, Brad Cloepfil, Simon Critchley, Sarah Williams Goldhagen, Stephanie Goto, Mathieu Lehanneur, Ibrahim Mahama, Toshiko Mori, Jasper Morrison, Paola Navone, Juhani Pallasmaa, Monique Péan, John Pawson, Ivy Ross, Aaron Schiller, and Billie Tsien. In truth, I could go on—there are far too many to mention here.

Thank you to Andrew Zuckerman. So much essential thinking from our conversations and work at The Slowdown has found its way into this book.

Thank you to Ghazaal Vojdani and Julia Novitch for the beautiful, tactile, wholly original book design. And to Keith Fox, Stephanie Holstein, and Emilia Terragni at Phaidon. It was a joy to create this with you. I'd also like to extend my appreciation to Belle Place, who worked with me on this book in its early stages, and to Mimi Hannon for the eagle-eye copy edits.

Thank you to Emma for your encouragement, love, and support.

Finally, I'd like to thank my family: Dad, Brandon, and Trent, and especially my great aunt Martha, a former city planner in Boston and Providence whose interest in—and enthusiasm for—urban design, architecture, cities, literature, history, and journalism entered my psyche at some point during my high school and college years, transformed me, and has never left. If there's anyone this book is dedicated to, it's her.

About the Author

Spencer Bailey is a writer, editor, and journalist. Co-founder of the media company The Slowdown and host of the Time Sensitive podcast, he has written at length about architecture, art, culture, and design for publications such as *Town & Country*, *The New York Times Magazine*, *Fortune*, *Newsweek*, and *Bloomberg Businessweek*. He is also the author of the book *In Memory Of: Designing Contemporary Memorials* (Phaidon, 2020). From 2013 to 2018, he was the editor-in-chief of *Surface* magazine. He lives in New York City.

Phaidon Press Limited
2 Cooperage Yard
London E15 2QR

Phaidon Press Inc.
65 Bleecker Street
New York, NY 10012

phaidon.com

First published 2023

ISBN 978 1 83866 391 9
ISBN 978 1 83866 664 4 (signed edition)

A CIP catalogue record for this book is available from the British Library and the Library of Congress.

Commissioning Editor: Emilia Terragni
Project Editor: Stephanie Holstein
Production Controller: Andie Trainer
Design: Ghazaal Vojdani and Julia Novitch